點心餃子書

Books by Eileen Yin-Fei Lo

The Chinese Banquet Cookbook: Authentic Feasts from China's Regions

China's Food (co-author)

Eileen Yin-Fei Lo's New Cantonese Cooking

From the Earth: Chinese Vegetarian Cooking

The Dim Sum Dumpling Book

點心餃子書

Eileen Yin-Fei Lo

Calligraphy by San Yan Wong

Macmillan • USA

MACMILLAN
A Simon & Schuster Macmillan Company
1633 Broadway
New York, NY 10019-6785

Library of Congress Cataloging-in-Publication Data

Lo, Eileen Yin-Fei.
The dim sum dumpling book / Eileen Yin-Fei Lo ; calligraphy by San Yan Wong.
p.   cm.
Includes index.
ISBN 0-02-090295-6
1. Cookery, Chinese. 2. Dim sum. 3. Dumplings. I. Title.
TX724.5.C5L59453   1995
641.5951—dc20   95-23095
CIP

Manufactured in the United States of America
10   9   8   7   6   5   4   3   2   1

Dedication and Acknowledgments

My family, after all, could not eat *all* of these dumplings and so, as I experimented, before deciding which pleased me most, the results went forth to students, neighbors, and friends.

A thank you is in order to those dim sum chefs, in Hong Kong and Canton particularly, who gave me so much encouragement and bits of their knowledge. My very special gratitude goes to my close friend, occasional teacher, and private calligrapher, San Yan Wong; to my agent, Carla Glasser, a persevering woman; to Justin Schwartz, my caring editor; and to Nahum Waxman, who continually pestered me to do this book.

But this book could not have been completed were it not for the patience and stomach capacities of my family, who together and individually sat through interminable tasting and testing sessions. We ate and argued and laughed, occasionally we fought, always we loved. Thank you Fred, Elena, Christopher, and Stephen.

Contents

Yum Cha: Teahouses and Memories

The earliest recollection I have of dim sum dumplings is of the time when I was four years old and lived in Siu Lo Cheun, or "Lo's Little Village," a town bearing my family's name in the suburban Cantonese region of Sun Tak.

My eighteen-year-old brother, Ching Mo, had won a rather large sum of money after many hours at the mah-jongg table, and he came bursting happily into our house, grabbed me by the hands, lifted me onto his shoulders, and shouted, "Let us go to *yum cha*!"

Now, *yum cha* means literally to "drink tea," but I knew he was not just going to treat me to a cup of *bo lei cha,* prized though it was. *Yum cha* meant to drink tea, but it also meant to "eat dim sum," the different and delicious small teahouse dumplings and wrapped foods that we loved so much. To eat dim sum in our family was quite a treat. Dim sum dumplings were customarily not made in the home: They were teahouse foods, and for us they were doubly a treat because the only teahouse in Siu Lo Cheun, like most other Cantonese teahouses, was only for men.

The teahouse was where men came to talk with other men about the buying and selling of land, about sugarcane crops and farming, about the fish they had caught and those they missed. They read their newspapers and conducted business, and those who were retired or wealthy enough not to have to work would bring their pet birds, in elaborate cages, and spend mornings in the teahouse at leisure. They would drink their pots of tea and, when the urge or need would come upon them, gesture for a small plate of those dumplings, or these, to be brought so as to enjoy them with their tea.

It was not exactly that women were forbidden to go into teahouses— it was just that they *did not*, by tradition. Even somewhat liberated women like my mother, Miu How, one of the very few women of Sun Tak to refuse the traditional foot bindings of upper-class females, would not go into a teahouse. Once a girl became ten years old or so, the teahouse became out of bounds. Goggle-eyed little girls of four, simultaneously happy and apprehensive, like me, however, were allowed in simply because they were little.

I remember the teahouse in Siu Lo Cheun as being one big room with many windows and many tables scattered about, all of them occupied by men. Memories of the room are vague, but memories of what I ate are vivid because I always ate the same things when my brother took me there: *char siu bau*, soft, fluffy, steamed, dough buns filled with small pieces of seasoned roast pork; *Har Gau*, half-moon-shaped dumplings filled with chopped shrimp; *siu mai*, basket-shaped dumplings of minced shrimp, pork, and mushrooms; and *pai gwat siu mai*, tiny morsels of spare ribs in a black bean sauce. To this day they are my favorite dim sum dumplings.

When I was twelve and left Siu Lo Cheun for Hong Kong, I went into a different world. Teahouses were social centers and many of them were vast, barnlike, multistoried restaurants that were places for families, including women. They were where you went during the New Year holiday, for the Dragon Boat Festival days of May, for the August Moon, often for birthdays, and almost always on Sundays.

My mother and father had sent me away from our town during the New Year school vacation in 1950 because of the revolution in China. They would not leave their home and lands but they wanted their daughter safe in Hong Kong. They were correct. I was spared the violence but not the sorrow, however, because my brother, who had taken me to the teahouse when I was four, died in Siu Lo Cheun's corner of that revolution two years after I left.

I lived in Kowloon, a city across from Hong Kong Island, for a while with a distant aunt, my father's number-five sister, and I remember going to the Nathan Tea House, one of those big places, more than once. I do not remember exactly what it looked like, but my feeling is that I did not care what it looked like, because it was where I could get those *char siu bau* that I loved. And I did. Subsequently I lived with a consortium of cousins out in the New Territories area of Fanling, about twenty miles from Kowloon. Our teahouse there was modest, but occasionally I got to go out to Tai Po as a chaperon to one of my cousins and her young man friend. The teahouse there was bigger, with a wider variety of dim sum dumplings, and though I did not particularly care about being a chaperon, the food, I remember, was very, very good.

It was back to Kowloon and the home of Luk Gu Cheh, my "number-six aunt," my father's younger sister, where I lived with her and three of her six children until I came to the United States. By the time I came to live with Luk Gu Cheh, one of her daughters had married and moved to England, and two others had their own apartments, but on rare occasions those daughters still in Hong Kong and her son, David, and I would assemble on a Sunday morning in one of Hong Kong's big dim sum restaurants and drink tea, eat dumplings, talk about our jobs, and gossip about our family and friends. I should say that it was my aunt Luk Gu Cheh—a splendid cook, filled with the tradition of fine cooking that permeates Sun Tak (where it is said the finest cooks in China come from)—who taught me much.

I had begun cooking at the age of five, learning a bit from my mother, but mostly from my father, Pak Wan, and my grandmother, Ah Paw. My grandmother was imperious, issuing orders to her cooks and to her daughters, but her knowledge was great. My father was a marvelous, meticulous cook. While quite young I was taught steaming and stir-frying, and the elements that in combination make for flavor. It was my father who insisted that I take each individual bean sprout, for example, and break off its ends so that the spring rolls he was teaching me to create would contain only the crunchy white centers of the sprout. Oh, how I hated doing that! It seemed to be a chore that took hours.

Because going to our teahouse was a rare event, we cooked a good many of what are classical dim sum preparations at home. At the age of seven I made *dai gut yau gor,* "good luck dumplings," before the Chinese New Year, and a year later I made my first turnip cake, which I remember eating with pickled red ginger. I also learned to make water dumplings, with their wonderful texture of pork, shrimp, and crisp bamboo shoots. It was I who went to the town bakery to buy the freshest bread with which to make shrimp toasts. I learned many dumpling preparations from Luk Gu Cheh and I continued to make many of them in the United States. In fact, I teach dim sum cookery now at the China Institute in America, in New York, and with each class it becomes a more enjoyable science as my students discover that they can fashion handsome dumplings and become, in effect, apprentice artists in the Chinese teahouse tradition. And I know, because they tell me, that they go into many dim sum dumpling restaurants, their families trailing after them, confident in their ability to judge and enjoy a food that once was a total mystery.

Even today, in the teahouses of Hong Kong and in the dim sum restaurants that have sprung up in other countries, it is not an uncommon sight to see four generations of a Chinese family around a *yum cha* table, drinking tea, eating uncountable varieties of dim sum, and chattering, their table converted instantly into a family reunion. True, there are still quite traditional teahouses, certainly in Canton and Hong Kong, and while some historic teahouses have vanished—places like Hing Wan in Hong Kong that provided racks from which the wealthy at leisure could hang their bird cages while they drank tea and ate dumplings—dim sum restaurants continue to proliferate and these days they are for shopgirls as much as they are for businessmen. Dim sum is for everybody.

Perhaps because of the misty rosiness that surrounds the history of tea, those dumplings and small wrapped bundles of food that accompany tea have emerged as a most romantic aspect of Cantonese cuisine, the most sophisticated style of Chinese cooking. Even the name dim sum is soft and lovely. Dim sum literally translated means "a point on the heart" or "a dot on the heart," and its gastronomic interpretation has come to be "a delight of the heart" or "a touch of the heart's delight." Lu Yu would like any of these.

A FEW WORDS ABOUT TEA

Lu Yu is China's historical Master of Tea, who in the eighth century wrote his *Classic of Tea,* which set down for the first time how tea leaves should be grown and processed, how tea should be brewed and steeped, how it should be presented and served, and how to create a tea caddie. Tea, Lu Yu wrote, was a drink for both the body and the soul, a mental stimulant, perhaps a way to immortality. And from his work all manner of tea observances proceeded.

Of course tea had been part of Chinese historical myth before Lu Yu's time. For example, some believe that tea was the serendipitous discovery of the Emperor Shen Nung during the third century B.C. How? Well, it seemed the emperor liked his drinking water boiled, and one day as it was aboil, a camellia blossom fell into it. The aroma was captivating and compelled him to taste the first pot of tea ever made. To this day the Chinese add camellias, rose and orange blossoms, the flowers of the lychee and the orange tree, and various other petals to tea.

Generally, it is believed that tea was first cultivated in China with bushes brought back from India by a Han Dynasty scholar in the second century, but evidence exists that tea as a soul-satisfying substance was very much a part of Chinese life before that time. Those who dispute the India theory suggest that tea, as a cultivated bush, originated in Hunan, later in Szechuan, as a member of the camellia family. What has emerged as the lore of Chinese tea, however, began with Lu Yu, who decreed that tea should be in cakes, that a bit of salt should be added to the boiling water used to boil the tea, and that brewed tea should be served only in bowls of underglase blue. Tea later was ground into powder; still later, dried leaves, after roasting to seal in the flavor, were used as the basis for pots of tea. And tea became a drink for all of the people, not just for the privileged.

These days most tea drunk in China and Hong Kong, and elsewhere, is brewed from little curled and dried leaves, although powdered teas and those in brick form are used occasionally. And though the Chinese have never developed an elaborate, ritualistic tea ceremony as have the Japanese, they do follow the dictates of Lu Yu, rules that in practical terms result in the best tea making.

Lu Yu said to place an earthenware vessel on a smokeless fire of charcoal, not just any charcoal as you might suppose, but charcoal made from olive pits. Water from a slow-moving stream should be put into the pot and boiled. Rushing water was bad for the throat, he said, and still water was not even to be considered. Once boiled, the water should be poured over the tea leaves in a porcelain cup. Most of the water should then be poured out, and fresh water added. Only then is the tea drinkable. He then suggested that it be drunk in the company of beautiful women in a pavilion next to a water lily pond or near a lacquered bridge.

Few of us have pavilions or water lily ponds or lacquered bridges, but we can brew tea well enough to enjoy it thoroughly. Water for tea should be drawn fresh from the tap (slow moving) and then boiled until the first bubbles appear. The teapot (earthenware) should be preheated with boiling water, then the leaves, one teaspoon of loose tea per person and one for the pot, should be placed in it. Pour the boiling water in and allow it to steep three to six minutes, the longer the stronger; then serve in porcelain cups.

From the hundreds of teas that are available in Chinese food and herbal shops, and from shops such as Fortnum & Mason in London, which was founded on a base of Chinese tea importing, have come the teas that are most familiar to the teahouse. They are:

Lung ching is a green tea, often called "Dragon Well," that is grown on the hillsides around Hangzhou, and it is regarded as the crowning achievement of Chinese tea-growing. It is served regularly in China at state dinners, is quite costly, and must be drunk when it is only a few months old. It does not keep, and after a year it loses every bit of its character, which is fresh, light, and green. The Chinese say that lung ching stimulates the appetite and is also a perfect remedy for the body when it is suffering from an excess of "hot elements"—dry mouth and throat, dry nostrils, and red eyes—which accurately describes running a fever. I also use Dragon Well tea to make tea-smoked duck. It imparts an absolutely breathtaking smokiness to the meat.

So mei is a strong, unfermented tea. The leaves are hand-picked, massaged between the palms, and wind-dried, never in the sun. Once brewed the tea has what some consider a pleasantly bitter taste. The Chinese regard so mei as quite good for respiration and for the relief of bronchial complications.

Bo lei, the tea of my childhood and a favorite of the Cantonese, seems to get better as it gets older. In Hong Kong it is possible to buy hundred-year-old cakes of bo lei. The Cantonese love bo lei with their dim sum dumplings because it is perfect, they believe, for digestion and as an ulcer preventative. It has a hearty and robust taste.

Jasmine is a clean-tasting tea that cleanses the palate and goes quite well with highly flavored or spicy foods. In general it is the tea of choice in most dim sum restaurants in the West. Made from dried flowers mixed with tea leaves it is, according to the Chinese, a fine remedy for a stomachache.

Chrysanthemum tea, made only from dried flowers, is believed to keep the palate clear. It tastes subtlety of the flower from which it is made and is supposed to be very good for the liver, the nerves, and the eyes. It will, the Chinese believe, ease headaches and toothaches and will reduce the body's temperature.

Soi sin is one of the many *oolong* teas favored in China. It comes from Fukien Province, is greenish-brown in color, and tastes slightly bitter. Some Chinese use it as a morning wake-up tea, as well as with their morning dumplings.

Teet koon yum, which is the Cantonese pronunciation of *teh kuan yin,* is the name of China's mythological Iron Goddess of Mercy. This is another of the oolongs and it derives its name from its dark, metallic green color. Actually, it is very similar to soi sin and is regarded as a stimulant. It is this very potent tea that is drunk by the southern Cantonese people known as the Chiu Chow, who favor its strength, in tiny cups, to create an appetite before meals and to clear the system of residual fat after eating.

Luk on is a black tea that looks quite strong but actually is very mild after it is brewed. It was called "Cloud Mist" and is highly regarded by the elderly whose digestion, it is said, cannot abide the stronger teas.

Green teas such as Dragon Well and so mei are not fermented, they are dried; while black teas like bo lei and luk on are made from fermented leaves that oxidize and turn black during the drying process. The oolongs are a combination of the two processes, the fermentation process being interrupted so that the leaves become dark black-green. The flower teas are generally green teas to which flowers and petals are added.

Tea, Lu Yu suggested, is a wonder, "if one is feeling hot, given to melancholia, suffering from aching of the brain, smarting of the eyes, trouble in the forelimbs, or afflicted in one hundred joints, he may take tea four or five times a day, the liquor is like the sweetest dew of heaven." And tea marries beautifully with food, particularly dim sum.

Imagine yourself in the Luk Yu Teahouse on Stanley Street in Hong Kong, a teahouse bearing the Cantonese version of Lu Yu's name. It is surely the most splendid of the traditional Chinese teahouses, almost three-quarters of a century old, with carved blackwood furniture, marble-topped tables, slowly circulating ceiling fans, screens, booths enclosed by carved wood walls, and exquisitely etched glass. You have come in, gone up to the second floor because it is more quiet than the street level, seated yourself, and asked for a pot of bo lei or jasmine tea. It is brought, along with teacups and a bowl a bit larger than a rice bowl. You pour some tea into the bowl and then roll each of the teacups through it, using the boiled tea to cleanse your cups. The bowl is removed and you pour your tea into the teacups and you sip and wait.

Soon you hear the singsong, "*har gau, siu mai, h-a-r g-a-u, si-u ma-i,*" the women's voices call out softly as these *dim sum mui*, the "dim sum maids," wheel carts among the tables, calling out what is in the steamers and pots. "*Pai gwat siu mai, woo gok, pa-i gw-at si-u ma-i, w-oo-oo g-ok.*" The maid does not ask if you want what she has, and she will serve the dim sum dumplings in tiny dishes or bamboo steamers only if you call out, or point to what she has on her cart.

It goes on. "*Char siu bau, yung hai kim, soi gau. Ch-ar si-u b-au, yung ha-i k-im, s-oi g-au.*"

You eat. You sample. The dishes pile up. Your teapot is empty. So you flip the lid backward so it rests on the handle and your waiter knows to bring a fresh pot of tea. Perhaps as he pours you are talking. There is no need to thank him with speech; you need only tap four fingers of your hand on the tabletop and he will acknowledge that you have thanked him with the unobtrusive etiquette of the teahouse.

And the dumplings!

Half-moons of pastry, tiny steamed dough baskets, buns filled with aromatic curried meats, triangles of fresh bean curd, pancakes studded with scallions, tiny pillows filled with shrimp, crescents filled with soup, dumplings like corkscrews, horns, rolls, cylinders, balls of meat dotted with pearls of rice, other buns filled with sweet pastes; the shapes and textures and tastes seem endless as they pass in wondrous parade.

The beginnings of the informal and variegated dim sum meal go back to the Sun dynasty, according to some historians, when tenth-century travelers along the highways of southern China began stopping at small roadside teahouses to refresh themselves with light meals and tea en route to their destinations. But centuries were required before the practice could take root, because two hundred years earlier, during Lu Yu's time, tea was really not an accompaniment to food, or vice versa. It was pure, a serene drink, a contemplative liquid, usually drunk quietly in private.

But the very practical discoveries of the benefits of tea upon diet, its aid as a digestive, its ability to cleanse the palate, its very real fat- and oil-cutting properties, soon made a marriage. Tea and food came together and the brief meal in the teahouse came soon after. And the foods evolved, as do most things in China, out of a combined mythological and historical perspective. A poet once threw himself into a river in protest and his supporters tossed rice and meat wrapped bamboo leaves after him. These were called jongtzu and a Cantonese version, *nor mai gai,* is served to this day in teahouses.

Then there is *dai gut yau gor*, which literally are "New Year's Horns," also called "good luck dumplings," and are made of brown sugar, pulverized peanuts, and sesame seeds. And there was the petty official named Kuai who ordered the death of a popular soldier. In protest people put together two sticks of dough and put them in oil, calling them *yau jai kuai,* "oil-fried kuai." Today they are found in teahouses and are considered Chinese crullers.

Historically and gastronomically, dim sum was at one time barely known in the northern centers of China. It was primarily a Cantonese phenomenon, and to this day it remains so. However, knowledge of dim sum and its limitless repertoire of dumplings, and love of them, has spread to all parts of China, and today there are dim sum dumplings in

Szechuan and Hunan in the west, and in Shanghai and Beijing in the north. In Shanghai in particular there has been an increase in the number and variety of dim sum, and in the region's cities of Hangzhou and Suzhou, dumplings are true culinary art.

Shanghai is in many ways the place where all of the cuisine of China came together, particularly during that time when it became the center for Western trading and investment. The scallion pancake is a Shanghai creation, and most dim sum pastries are from Shanghai, evolutions and adoptions of Western cakes and pastries. Soup buns are from Shanghai and so are the *wor tip*, those very popular dumplings known as potstickers. Of more recent Shanghai vintage are so-called Shanghai street dumplings, *sueng hoi gai bin gau*, or *bau jai*, so-called "little buns," basically smaller size potstickers. All of these are familiar in today's dim sum restaurants.

In the early days of the Chinese revolution, when many Chinese fled to Hong Kong and Taiwan for refuge, they brought with them foods and food traditions. Shanghai refugees, for example, created dumplings that they cooked over small burners on the street and sold to make a living. Today these dumplings are dim sum restaurant staples. These émigrés would set up small charcoal-fed stoves and pan fry their potstickers and their street dumplings. Over the years many of these street sellers have become restaurateurs.

Dim sum, however, remains basically Cantonese, and Hong Kong, a Cantonese city, is surely the world center for dim sum. Its teahouses are large, good-natured restaurants that are hospitable, noisy, often boisterous with celebrations of all sorts, and redolent with the continually changing aromas of freshly made dumplings. Families, friends, and business acquaintances sit around vast circular tables, talking and eating, arguing, baiting, and teasing, ordering from the maid when the mood strikes them. The Cantonese like to talk, often all of them together it seems, and in the dim sum teahouses that is what they to. But they also eat—bountifully—and they drink tea, much tea, all of it to delight the heart.

But dim sum and its dumplings are no longer confined to Hong Kong, nor to China. Its traditions have spread throughout the West and these days there is no country, no city, and few towns without restaurants serving dim sum, either in the traditional manner of a relaxed morning meal, breakfast, or brunch, or dim sum served as the first course in larger meals. The dim sum kitchen is most adaptable. It knows no limits.

A dim sum master chef, a *dai see fu*, is an honored member of the broad Chinese kitchen, a person in great demand, who can create on any day an infinite number of varieties on the theme of the dim sum dumpling. This is what I urge you to do. Adapt the recipes in this book, with fillings of your own liking, with shapes of your own fancy, and with your own design. Always enjoy. *Ho ho sik,* the Cantonese say— good eating.

Chapter 1

The Dim Sum Kitchen

TOOLS AND TECHNIQUES

I hear repeatedly, from different people, that although they love Chinese food, the very idea of preparing it in their own kitchens frightens them, dim sum more so. Why? Because, they confess, the use of the somewhat alien wok and cleaver is mysterious, and the idea of sculpting dough is something better left to the experts. They repeat tales they have heard about the tediousness of hours of cutting and slicing so something can be cooked in a very few minutes. They would rather enjoy their stir-fries and their dim sum in restaurants.

Well, on one level they are correct. Fine Chinese food of all schools and of all varieties can surely be enjoyed in today's sophisticated restaurants. On another level they are *so* wrong. Not to cook Chinese food— certainly one of the most creative and varied cuisines in the world—at home is to cheat yourself out of the unbelievable satisfaction and well-being that comes with creation. Chinese cuisine, perhaps more than any other, is constantly changing, being added to and altered by the talents of its practitioners.

There really is no mystery; there is only learning. Any feelings of mystery vanish once you learn how, and learning the techniques of Chinese cuisine—in our particular case, the ways of dim sum and the teahouse—will be anything but tedious. What you will experience instead is delight as you learn. I am confident of this because I share it over and over again with my students.

Tedious?

It seems to me that a couple of hours spent to prepare something that will be both beautiful to contemplate and delicious to taste, that will delight you and your guests, is not tedious. When what you have prepared brings a certain joy, and smiles of satisfaction to the faces of those who are enjoying your efforts, is that not a wonderful reward? I think it is.

This is the sort of feeling I have tried to impart to my students through the years. It is not just biting into a dumpling that yields a mouthful of flavorful broth, brewed especially for this dumpling, for example, that is satisfying. The process itself should be satisfying—the preparation of the dough, the hard work that fashions a rounded dumpling, its aromas as it steams. It is as wonderful as the finished dish.

The key to such enjoyment is, of course, to do things correctly and with economy. If you do not prepare your ingredients and utensils properly, then any cookery will become overpowering and frustrating— Chinese cuisine perhaps more so because it demands a certain discipline. Yet Chinese cooking generally, and dim sum cooking in particular, can be free of any concerns if you tend to basics.

"Basics" means not only becoming familiar with individual food-stuffs and spices, but learning the techniques to be used in dealing with them as well as the properties and capacities of the tools necessary to work with them. If you consider the number and variety of dumplings that exist in dim sum cookery, an art that is constantly being added to, it is surprising and gratifying for most people to learn that only a few special utensils are required to prepare them. Following are those that you will need, and you will undoubtedly find that most of the others you need are already in your kitchen:

Wok
Wok ring
Wok cover
Wok brush
Chinese spatula

Chinese mesh strainer
Bamboo steamers
Bamboo chopsticks
Chinese cleaver

Cooking with the Wok

In a cuisine so steeped in tradition as is Chinese, there is nothing more traditional than the wok. It is a thousand-year-old Chinese creation, first made of iron, later of carbon steel, still later of aluminum, shaped like an oversized soup plate. Its concave shape, which places its belly right into a flame or heat source, makes it an all-purpose cooker ideal for stir-frying, for pan-frying, deep-frying, blanching, and steaming. It is a perfect vessel in which to make sauces as well.

It is, in carbon steel, about as close to perfection as you can get in a cooking utensil. Though it is neither a pot nor a pan, it functions as both. Its shape permits foods to be tossed rapidly through the hot oil in its well without becoming greasy. That same shape permits it conversion into a large steamer simply by using a cover or tiers of bamboo steamers. Much of the attraction for the wok these days is derived from the realization that wok cooking is natural cooking.

If you buy one wok it should be made of carbon steel. Though not at all pretty when it is new, because of its coating of heavy, sticky oil, the carbon steel wok, cleaned and seasoned, is ideal and will last for years. It comes in various sizes, but for our purpose a wok fourteen inches in diameter will be perfect.

Once bought, it should be washed in extremely hot water with a bit of liquid detergent. The inside should be cleansed with a sponge, the outside with steel wool and cleanser; then it should be rinsed and, still wet, placed over a fire, and dried with a paper towel to prevent instant rust. With the wok still over a burner, one teaspoon of peanut oil should be tipped into its bowl and rubbed around with a paper towel. This oiling should be repeated until the towel is free of any traces of black residue. Your wok is then ready.

What I usually do with a new wok is make a batch of French-fried potatoes as a first cooking task. That is the perfect way to season a wok. I put in four cups of peanut oil, heat it until I see wisps of white smoke rising, then put the potatoes in. Most household stoves will not support the curved belly of a wok steadily. But a **wok ring,** a circle of carbon steel, set atop the burner will do nicely.

After that first washing of your wok, detergents should *never* be used in its bowl. It should be washed with extremely hot water, scrubbed perhaps with a stiff **wok brush** (inexpensive and usually available where you buy your wok) or a sponge. After rinsing, it should be dried quickly with a paper towel, then placed over a flame for thorough drying. If you have finished cooking in it for the day, then it should be reseasoned with a bit of peanut oil rubbed around the inside with a paper towel. This should be done for at least the first fifteen to twenty uses of the wok until it becomes shiny and dark-colored, which indicates that it is completely seasoned.

If the wok is to be used several times in the course of one cooking session, then it should be washed, wiped with a paper towel, and dried over heat after each use.

The wok is indispensable for dim sum cookery. All of its capabilities are used: It is used to stir-fry the various dumpling fillings; to deep-fry such delicacies as spring rolls, shrimp toasts, and stuffed crab claws; to oil blanch vegetables and meats so they retain their flavor and juices; to water blanch, which effectively removes water from vegetables and meats but does not dry them out; and finally, for steaming—which is truly the cornerstone of dim sum cooking.

Stir-Frying

For stir-frying you will need a **Chinese spatula,** a shovel-shaped tool available either in carbon steel or in stainless steel, of various sizes. I prefer one that is medium-sized. Stir-frying is by far the most dramatic of Chinese cooking techniques. It is fascinating to watch finely sliced and chopped foods being whisked through a touch of oil and tossed about the wok with a spatula. Hands and arms move, and the wok is often tipped back and forth. Stir-frying seems to be all movement. But mostly it is preparation.

The object of stir-frying is to cook vegetables exactly to the point at which they retain their flavor, color, crispness, and nutrition. Meat is generally shredded or thinly sliced and seared so that its juices are kept in. To do this you must prepare all of the elements of your dish before stir-frying. This is particularly the case with dumpling fillings, which *must* retain their flavors.

Vegetables, for example, finely cut, must be next to the wok, ready to be put into the hot oil, and the meat and shellfish that are to accompany them. This is simply organization, so that as you cook you will have everything within your reach and the rhythm of the stir-fry will not be interrupted.

To stir-fry: Heat the wok for a specified time. Pour the oil into the wok and coat its sides by spreading the oil with a spatula. When a wisp of white smoke appears place the foods in the wok, in order, and toss them through the oil with the spatula. If the vegetables are too wet they will not stir-fry well, so they should be patted dry with paper towels. If they are too dry, however, you may have to sprinkle a few drops of water with your hand into the wok while cooking. When water is sprinkled in this manner bits of steam are created, which aid in the cooking process. Meats are generally stir-fried for about three to four minutes and shellfish, particularly shrimp, are stir-fried for one to two minutes, until their color changes.

Stir-frying may appear initially as a rather frenzied activity, but it really isn't, and the more you do the more you will realize that it is simply a matter of establishing a rhythm.

Deep-frying: The object of deep-frying is to cook food through inside while the outside becomes golden and lightly crusty. Most of the savory dumplings of dim sum are fried in this manner.

When I wish to make my wok into a deep fryer, I heat it briefly then place four to six cups of peanut oil inside, and heat the oil to 325°F to 375°F, depending upon what I am cooking. The oil should be heated to a temperature a bit higher than that required for frying the food, because when food is placed in it, the oil temperature will drop. For example, when I wish to deep-fry dumplings at 325°F, I heat oil to 350°F, then place the dumplings in. The temperature drops, then rises again, and I use a frying thermometer (which I leave in the oil) to regulate the oil heat.

Softer dim sum, such as *woo gok,* need oil heated to 350°F to 375°F; dumplings of thicker dough cook at from 325°F to 350°F. When the oil reaches the proper temperature, slide the food from the inside edge of the wok into the oil. I suggest you cook only a few dumplings at a time (the recipes are specific) until you become more expert. Cook them until the color and crispness satisfy you, turning them over as they cook. They will usually cook thoroughly, and properly, in three to five minutes. Remember to keep the temperature of the oil steady by turning the heat up or down as required. The utensil to use for deep-frying is the **Chinese mesh strainer**, a circular steel-mesh strainer attached to a long, flat bamboo handle. I prefer one ten inches in diameter. There are also stainless steel strainers, flat and round, with holes punched through. These work quite nicely if you prefer them.

Oil blanching: This relatively simple cooking technique is basically a sealing process. Its aim is to seal in the flavor of foods, and in the case of vegetables, retain their bright color. Foods to be blanched are placed on the mesh of the strainer and lowered into the oil for specified times. These are determined by the individual recipes in this book. When foods are removed from the oil, the excess oil should be drained and the oil blanched foods set aside until used.

Water blanching: This method removes water from foods and makes for lighter dim sum fillings. In particular, vegetables are enhanced by water blanching. They are placed in boiling water to which baking soda has been added, and their color brightens. When removed from the water their color is retained.

Dietitians contend that water blanching with baking soda removes some of the vitamins from vegetables. What I can say is that the technique has been used for centuries in China, and to this day is widely used throughout European kitchens, particularly in France and Italy. The Italians claim that baking soda is advantageous for the stomach. So I say, take your choice.

Steaming: Chinese steamers are round, usually made of bamboo, but they can also be made of aluminum. In addition, you can buy small, individual steamers of made of bamboo or stainless steel. Steamers come in various sizes but I prefer those twelve inches in diameter. They can be stacked two or three high and topped with a cover of woven bamboo. In general, foods steam better in bamboo, but metal is easier to maintain. It's your choice.

Steaming is almost a life-giving process. Dough becomes soft, light dumplings and buns when subjected to steam's wet, penetrating heat. Food that is dried becomes moist, that which is shrunken, expands. Steaming preserves flavor and bestows, particularly to dough, a glistening coat.

It is an artful technique as well, because foods can be placed in lovely arrangements within bamboo steamers and, once cooked, they can be served without being disturbed. Steaming requires virtually no oil, except that used to coat the bamboo reeds at the bottom of the steamers to prevent sticking. Large vegetable leaves such as lettuce, cabbage, or bok choy can even be used as liners, thus eliminating any need for oil. If you use a leaf, lightly water blanch it first.

To steam, place 6 cups of water in a wok, the usual amount, and bring it to a boil. Place steamers in the wok so that they sit evenly above, but not touching, the water. Depending upon the number and size of the dim sum dumplings to be steamed, you will be able to stack as many as three steamers, covering the top, and the contents of all will cook beautifully. Most steamed dim sum cook thoroughly in 7 to 12 minutes. Steamed rice requires 25 to 35 minutes. Cakes require steaming for 1 to 1½ hours. Boiling water should be on hand at all times during the steaming process, to replace any water that may evaporate from the wok.

The new countertop steamers work well for steaming dumplings as well. You will still need to coat the inside of the steamer lightly with oil or line it with a blanched cabbage or lettuce leaf, as explained above.

Tempering: Occasionally dim sum are placed within steamers in porcelain or Pyrex dishes to cook and to serve on. These dishes must first be seasoned, or tempered, so they will not crack.

Fill your wok with six cups of cold water. Place a cake rack inside and pile up dishes to be prepared on the rack, making certain they are completely covered by the cold water. Cover with a **wok cover** (usually of aluminum, shaped like either a drum or a dome, it seals the contents of the wok) and bring the water to a boil. Let the water boil for ten minutes, turn off the heat, and allow the wok to cool to room temperature. The dishes are then seasoned and can be placed in steamers without fear that they will crack. As an alternative to tempering you may use stainless steel or aluminum bowls.

Working with the Cleaver

If the wok is an all-purpose cooker, then the cleaver comes close to being the perfect all-purpose cutting instrument. The Chinese kitchen would not be a kitchen without the broad-bladed, wood-handled cleaver, and nobody who cooks Chinese food should be without one. Rather formidable-looking, the cleaver occasionally frightens people who think that the first time they use it they will slice off one or more of their fingers. This is, of course, nonsense.

The cleaver, when held correctly so that its weight and balance will be well used, can do virtually anything a handful of lesser knives can. It slices, shreds, threads, dices, minces, and chops, all with great ease. It mashes, it is a scoop, it can function as a dough scraper, and it even serves as a work surface for a limited number of dim sum dumplings.

Cleavers come in various sizes and weights, suitable for every use from mincing to butchering. An all-purpose cleaver I recommend for this book is one that weighs about three-quarters of a pound, is about eight inches long, and has a blade about three and a half inches wide. The best is produced by Dexter, and is made of stainless steel.

Different people hold cleavers in different ways, and much is made of the "proper" way to hold one. But there is no single way to hold the cleaver. It should be held comfortably and in such a way as to make the weight of the blade work efficiently and firmly. I use two basic grips.

The first is for chopping and mincing. I grip the handle in a fistlike grasp and swing straight down in short and controlled strokes. The wrist dictates the force.

The second is for slicing, shredding, and dicing. I grip the handle as before, but permit the index finger to stretch out along the side of the flat blade to give it guidance. The wrist, which barely moves with this grip, is virtually rigid and almost becomes an extension of the cleaver, as the blade is drawn across the food to be cut. When you use this grip your other hand becomes a guide. Your fingertips should anchor the food to be cut and your knuckle joints should guide the cleaver blade, which will brush them ever so slightly as it moves across the food.

In most dim sum preparations vegetables and meats are sliced, shredded, or diced. Garlic, occasionally ginger, and shrimp are generally minced.

A cleaver, if it is made of carbon steel, should be washed and dried quickly to prevent rust. Under no circumstances should it be placed in a dishwasher. If your cleaver should show a spot of rust, it should be rubbed off with steel wool, dried, and touched with a bit of vegetable oil.

> Note: Most kitchens these days contain heavy-duty electric mixers equipped with dough hooks. The amounts of dough for dumplings in this book are too small for use with an electric mixer so I do not use one, or recommend one. All of the dough can be kneaded by hand.

A food processor is another ubiquitous appliance. I use it only sparingly in dim sum cookery, mainly to mash difficult dumpling fillings such as lotus seeds and red beans. These fillings are available in cans. Except for these fillings, a processor is not necessary for the recipes in this book.

FOODS

Dim sum and its dumplings constitute a specialized Chinese cuisine and require some ingredients not readily available at your local supermarket. Not as many as you might imagine, however. Most of the foodstuffs of Chinese origin are nevertheless easily obtainable at Chinese and other Asian groceries, and I have noticed with some gratification that more and more specialty food shops as well as larger general-purpose markets are stocking the foods used in Chinese cookery.

For dim sum dumplings, with their accent on the fashioning of dough, you will need the customary ingredients necessary in baking, such as baking powder, baking soda, vegetable shortenings, dried yeast, and of course, flour. There seems no need to list all of the paraphernalia of baking since most of it is common to most kitchens.

I have avoided listing products by brand name except for clarification and in instances where I feel the quality of a particular brand is quite superior. The primary exception is with flours. The flours I prefer are quite specific by brand, the result of much testing and baking under all seasonal and temperature conditions.

Here then are the foods you will need to make your dim sum dumplings:

BAMBOO SHOOTS

Though these come canned in various ways, I prefer bamboo shoots cut into large chunks, so that I can cut them to my own specifications. They are crisp and golden yellow and once removed from the can, they can be kept in glass jars or plastic containers. Refrigerated and kept in water that is changed daily, they will keep four to six weeks. Cans may also be labeled "winter bamboo shoots." These are a bit rougher in texture, but may be used.

BEAN CURD, FRESH

These come in square cakes, two and a half to three inches to a square. Made from soybeans, they are white and have a consistency somewhat like custard. I prefer the fresh, individual cakes rather than those that come several to a package, as they are sometimes sold. Bean curd is also known as *tofu*, a Japanese variation of the Chinese word for bean curd, *daufu*. Bean curd has little taste of its own and its versatility lies in its ability to absorb the tastes of other substances. Kept refrigerated in a container, bean curd will keep up to three weeks if the water in the container is changed daily. Soybean cake is bean curd that has been cooked in soy sauce and five-spice powder and comes packed in plastic bags in small cakes, and can be found in the refrigerated compartments of markets.

BEAN SPROUTS

These are white, plump, and crunchy and are grown from mung beans. They are sold by weight, and can be stored in plastic bags into which holes have been punched. Storage must be in the refrigerator and they can be kept no more than four days, after which they lose their color and firmness.

BLACK BEANS, FERMENTED

These beans, usually preserved in salt, are wonderfully fragrant and tasty. They come in plastic packages and in cans, some in packages seasoned slightly with orange peel and ginger. Before using, salt should be rinsed off. They can be kept for as long as a year, without refrigeration, as long as they are in a tightly sealed container.

BOK CHOY

This word is Cantonese for "white vegetable" and describes best the white-stalked, green-leafed vegetable that is so versatile and useful in the Chinese kitchen. It is sold by weight, its taste is sweet, and it is juicy. Although it is often called "Chinese cabbage," this is a misnomer because it is not at all like a cabbage. It will keep for about a week in the vegetable drawer of a refrigerator, but it tends to lose its sweetness quickly, so I recommend using it while fresh.

*BOK CHOY, TIENTSIN (SEE **Tientsin Bok Choy**, PAGE 31)*

CHINESE BLACK MUSHROOMS

These dried mushrooms come in boxes or in cellophane packs. They are black, dark gray, or speckled in color, and range in size from those with caps about the size of a nickel to those with diameters of three inches. Those in boxes are choicest, both in size and color, and, of course, are the more expensive. Chinese black mushrooms must always be soaked in hot water for at least thirty minutes before use, their stems removed and discarded, and they should be thoroughly cleaned on the underside of the cap and squeezed dry. In their dried form they will keep indefinitely in a tightly closed container, If you live in an especially damp or humid climate they should be stored in the freezer.

 *CHINKIANG VINEGAR (SEE VINEGAR, CHINKIANG, PAGE 31)*

 CHIVES, CHINESE

These are also known as "garlic chives." They are more pungent than the sort most Westerners are used to, and are wider and flatter, though of the same deep green color.

 CORIANDER, FRESH

This is also called "Chinese parsley" or "cilantro." It has a strong aroma and taste and, used either as a seasoning agent or as a garnish, it is distinctive. Often it is suggested that flat-leaf Italian parsley—which it resembles—be used as a substitute. There is *no* substitute for the herb. It should be used quickly so that its bouquet will be appreciated, but it can be kept refrigerated for a week to ten days.

CURRY POWDER

There are many brands of curry powder on the market. I prefer the stronger, more pungent brands from India. My favorite is Madras, from Bombay. Another brand, domestically packed, that I find satisfying is Crosse & Blackwell.

EGG ROLL SKINS

Food wrappers made of flour and water, often with egg added. For fuller explanation see the Spring Roll chapter of this book.

FIVE-SPICE POWDER

A mixture that imparts the distinctive taste of anise. It can be made from a combination of spices including star anise, fennel seeds, cinnamon, cloves, gingerroot, licorice, nutmeg, and Sichuan peppercorns. Obviously there are more than five spices listed, but different varieties use different combinations. However, anise and cinnamon dominate in all the blends.

FLOUR

There are many brands of flour available, but I have chosen three, after much testing, as ideal for dim sum dough. They are:

> Pillsbury Best Bread Flour, enriched, bromide, naturally white,
>   high protein, high gluten
> Pillsbury Best All-Purpose Flour, enriched, bleached
> Gold Medal All-Purpose Flour, enriched, bleached

The properties of all flours and dough are discussed at length in the Doughs for Dumplings section (pages 47–49) of the book.

GINGERROOT

You cannot do without ginger in Chinese cookery. When selecting gingerroots, look for those with smooth outer skins, because like many of us, ginger begins to wrinkle and roughen with age. It seasons, it is used to diffuse strong fish and shellfish odors, and the Chinese say that it greatly reduces stomach acidity. It is used rather sparingly and most often peeled and sliced before use. Placed in a heavy brown paper bag and refrigerated, it will keep from four to six weeks. I do not recommend trying to preserve it in wine or freezing it, because either way it loses its strength. Nor do I recommend powdered ginger or bottled ginger juice as cooking substitutes, because for ginger there is no substitute.

Young ginger, pinkish white, smooth, and crisp grows in two crops, one in late summer, and another in January and February in southern China. In the United States it is available from midspring to midfall and is often referred to, mistakenly, as spring ginger.

GINGER JUICE

This is easily made. Peel ginger and grate it on a small single-panel grater. Place in a garlic press and squeeze. This fresh juice is far better than any in jars. It may be kept for two days refrigerated.

GINGER PICKLE

Slices of young ginger are pickled with salt, sugar, and white vinegar. Here is my recipe:

Boil 1¹/₂ pounds fresh young ginger, washed thoroughly and cut into ¹/₈-inch slices, in 8 cups of water and 1 teaspoon baking soda. Drain well. Make a marinade of 1¹/₄ teaspoons salt, ⁵/₈ cup of white vinegar, and 1 cup of sugar. Add to ginger. Cover and refrigerate. The ginger pickle will keep for at least three months in a tightly closed glass jar.

If young ginger is unavailable, use regular ginger, but because older ginger is much stronger, use half the amount specified for young ginger in recipes.

GLUTINOUS RICE

Different from the usual white, long-grained rice, used so often in Chinese dishes. This is short-grained and when cooked, its kernels tend to stick together, which is why it is often called "sticky rice." Some packages of this rice are labeled "sweet rice."

HOISIN SAUCE

This chocolate-brown sauce is made from soybeans, garlic, sugar, and chilies. Some brands add a touch of vinegar, others are thickened with flour. It is best known as a complement to Peking Duck. It usually comes in jars. After opening it will keep refrigerated for many months.

JÍCAMA

Known as *sah gut* in China. It is a large, roundish root, shaped like a spin top. With crisp and sweet flesh, it is a favorite of the Chinese, and widely available in all kinds of markets. Jícama is also a fine substitute if you are unable to obtain fresh water chestnuts.

LOTUS SEED PASTE

This deep red-chocolate-colored paste is made from lotus seeds cooked with sugar. It comes in cans, of many brands, generally all of which are of good quality. Once removed from the can it will keep, refrigerated in a closed container, for an extended time.

OYSTER SAUCE

A somewhat thick sauce, the base of which is ground, dried oysters. This is used generously by the Chinese to add color to preparations and to accent flavors. It usually comes in bottles. It can be kept indefinitely, if refrigerated in its bottle. At room temperature, if used repeatedly, it will keep for at least a year.

RED BEAN PASTE

This deep-red paste, made by boiling red beans and sugar, comes in cans. Like lotus seed paste, most canned red bean pastes are of good quality. It is used for fillings in buns, pastries, and dumplings.

SAUSAGES, CHINESE

These *lop cheung* are traditionally made in China of pork, pork liver, and duck liver. Very little sausage with duck liver is available in the United States, however. Most common is pork sausage, usually in pairs, threaded through with pork fat, and held together with string. They are cured, but not cooked, and thus must be cooked before eating. They can be kept refrigerated for about a month, and frozen for two months. A somewhat leaner pork sausage from Canadian processors is also available in some markets, but in my view it lacks the defined flavor of the sausages made in the United States.

SESAME OIL

An aromatic oil with a strong, almost nutlike smell that is used both as a cooking oil and as an additive and a dressing. Adding a bit of it to an already prepared dish imparts a fine flavor. It is thick and brown when it comes from China and Japan, thinner and lighter from the Middle East. I recommend the former. It may be stored for many months at room temperature in a tightly capped bottle.

SESAME SEEDS

Both black and white seeds, either roasted or not, are generally used in dumpling fillings, as decorations, or as garnishes. They are also used in raw form as an ingredient and occasionally in the making of sweets as well. To prevent the seeds from becoming stale and unusable they may be stored in the freezer.

SHAO-HSING WINE

A sherrylike wine made and bottled in China and Taiwan. There are several grades. I use the basic wine, but also the best grade of *Shao-Hsing* (labeled *Hau Tiao Chiew* and pronounced "far jiu") for particular dishes. A good, dry sherry may be substituted.

SHRIMP, DRIED

These are small shrimp, dried and salted for preservation. Before using they should be soaked in warm water for at least thirty minutes. They will keep for two to three months in a tightly closed container kept in a dry place. They can also be frozen for storage if they are not used often. They should be orange-pink in color, and a sure sign that they are aging and losing their strength is their change to a grayish color.

SNOW PEA SHOOTS

The fine, tender tips of the vines on which snow peas grow. These leaves are quite sweet when cooked, and after being cooked and eaten happily by the Chinese for centuries, they have been recently "discovered" by Western chefs for their freshness and taste.

SOY SAUCE, LIGHT OR DARK

The light soys are usually taken from the top of the first batch of soy sauce being prepared; the darker soys later, from the bottom. Both are made of soybeans, flour, salt, and water. There are many brands, from many countries, but my favorite is Yuet Heung Yuen, made in Hong Kong. The light soy from this manufacturer is labeled "pure soybean sauce"; the dark soy is labeled "A" soy sauce; the so-called double dark soy is labeled "C" soy sauce, or simply double-dark. Dark soys are best with meats, for roasting, and for sauces, for rich and dark coloring. Light soys are best for shrimp, chicken, and pork, and the Chinese believe they give a sweet taste to these foods. I often combine the two soys for different tastes and colorings.

SPRING ROLL SKINS

These skins are cooked, thin and white in color, and contain no eggs. For a fuller explanation of the skins and their various brands, see the Spring Roll chapter of this book.

SZECHUAN MUSTARD PICKLE

This is also known as plain mustard pickle. It is made from Chinese radishes cooked with chili powder and salt. It can be added to soups and stir-fried with vegetables. It is never used fresh, only in its preserved form. It can be bought loose by weight, but more often is found in cans, labeled "Szechuan preserved vegetables" or "Sichuan mustard pickle."

There can be instances of loose labeling. Do not confuse this with "sour mustard pickle," which is preserved mustard greens. Use care when you buy. Once a can of Szechuan mustard pickle is opened, place in a glass jar. It will keep for one year, refrigerated.

TAPIOCA FLOUR

Often called tapioca starch, this is made from the starch of the cassava root, and much of it comes packaged from Thailand. It is used both as a basis for particular dim sum dough and as a thickener for sauces in many preparations as a substitution for cornstarch. I also use it for dusting in many preparations.

TARO ROOT

This starchy root of the tropical taro plant, which is called *poi* in Hawaii, is somewhat like a potato but is more fibrous and is tinged throughout with purple threads. It must be eaten cooked, usually steamed, and as it cooks it emits a chestnutlike aroma.

TIENTSIN BOK CHOY

Often called "celery cabbage," this comes in two varieties, either with a long stalk or a rounder sort that is much leafier. The latter is referred to most often as Tientsin bok choy, and I prefer it because it is the sweeter of the two. It is also at its best in the spring. It may be kept refrigerated in a plastic bag for about a week, but like bok choy, it tends to lose its sweetness, so I suggest using it early, if not at once.

VINEGAR, CHINKIANG

This very strong, aromatic red vinegar is used throughout southern China, not only in Canton and Hong Kong, but also among the Hakka and Chiu Chow people. It is very distinctive. Red wine vinegar may be substituted for it, but it is not a *true* substitute.

WATER CHESTNUTS

These grow in mud and water, but when washed off, peeled, and cleaned, they are the crunchiest of foods. They are available fresh, which is the most desirable, or canned. Fresh and unpeeled they will keep refrigerated and in a brown paper bag for four to six weeks. Canned water chestnuts will keep refrigerated, in water changed daily, in an airtight container for two to three weeks. I prefer fresh to canned. As a matter of fact, I prefer jícama over canned water chestnuts, if fresh water chestnuts are unavailable (see jícama, page 27).

WHEAT STARCH

This is what remains of wheat flour when the wheat's protein is removed to make gluten. This starch is the basis for several dumpling wrappings. It will keep for at least a year if placed in a tightly sealed container and kept in a dry place.

WON TON SKINS

These dumpling wrappers are uncooked, rolled-out wheat dumpling skins. They are used as alternates to wheat flour dough skins. For a full explanation of the many skins, see the Wheat Flour Dough section of this book, pages 64–65.

Chicken Broth

Many of the recipes in this book call for chicken broth. You may of course buy it canned, but here is a recipe for a fine-tasting broth, quite like a stock in its intensity, that will enhance your dim sum preparations. It is simple to make and can be kept for later use.

7 pounds chicken bones
10 cups water
4 quarts of cold water
1 piece fresh ginger (4 ounces), lightly smashed
4 cloves garlic, whole and peeled
4 scallions, ends discarded, cut into halves
4 medium onions, peeled, quartered
$^1/_2$ teaspoon white peppercorns, whole
Salt

Makes 8 cups

1. In a large pot bring the 10 cups of water to a boil. Add the chicken bones and allow to boil for 1 minute. This will bring blood and meat juices to the top. Turn off the heat, pour off the water, and run cold water over the bones to clean them.
2. Place the bones in a pot, add 4 quarts of cold water, the ginger, garlic, scallions, onions, and peppercorns, and salt to taste. Cover and bring to a boil; partially uncover, and allow the broth to simmer for 4 hours.
3. Strain the contents; reserve the liquid, discard the solid ingredients. Refrigerate until used.

Note: This broth will keep 2 to 3 days refrigerated, or it can be frozen. I recommend dividing it among small plastic containers, each holding 2 cups. They may be frozen for up to 3 months.

Chapter 2

A Collection of Sauces, Oils, and Dips

Dim sum, either in a restaurant or at home, can be the most informal of meals, served randomly, its dumplings set out in no particular order except to satisfy the desires of those eating. Just about the only rule is to eat sweets toward the end of the meal, but even that is a rule to be broken.

Dim sum can, however, be served formally, in individual porcelain dishes, or family style out of large platters or steamers. How you serve depends upon your taste and inclinations. These same whims dictate what sort of sauce, oil, or dip you might prefer with your dumplings. These accompaniments are usually presented in restaurants in tiny shallow dishes for dipping, and can be served at home in the same manner. These small dishes, often called "soy sauce dishes," are available widely. Each will hold about two teaspoons of whatever is your fancy.

In Canton the use of sauces, oils, and dips with dim sum dumplings, especially the variety that "heat the mouth," has traditionally been regarded as almost sinful, because the Cantonese believe that food perfectly prepared requires no enhancement. I recall when I was very little and went reaching for some hot oil to sprinkle on some spring rolls, my grandmother glared at me and stopped my hand in midair with a call of "Barbarian!"

These days however, the Cantonese, like most everybody else in other parts of China and in the West, use some sauces, oils, and dips for their dim sum dumplings, including a few that are spicy and hot. I have developed various sauces and oils over the years, which I use as accompaniments for specific dumplings. To be sure, there are a sufficient number of dishes and sauces for you to experiment with. I know that many of my students prefer their dim sum with dips that I would not dream of using, because I suspect my grandmother would again become angry with me. Nonetheless, I have become used to having some of these sauces, oils, and dips with my dim sum. I believe their use is but one more example of the adventure to be found in the world of dim sum.

Scallion Oil

Chung Yau

Scallion oil is less an accompaniment than it is an ingredient. It is used in recipes in this book, and is a base for other sauces.

> 3 bunches of scallions, washed, dried, ends
> cut off, each scallion cut into 4 pieces
> 3 cups of peanut oil

Makes 3 cups

1. Heat wok over medium heat. Add peanut oil, then add scallions. When the scallions turn brown, the oil is done. Strain the oil through a fine strainer into a bowl and allow it to cool to room temperature.
2. Pour the scallion oil into a glass jar and refrigerate until needed.

Note: Do not discard the scallions. When strained out of oil, place them in a plastic container and refrigerate. They keep indefinitely and are a fine addition to any soup you might make.

Tim Chung Yau

Sweet Scallion Sauce

¹/₄ cup Scallion Oil (page 36)
¹/₂ cup dark soy sauce
3 ¹/₂ tablespoons sugar
3 tablespoons cold water

Makes about 1 cup

1. Heat wok over medium heat. Pour in Scallion Oil, soy sauce, sugar, and water. Stir clockwise until all ingredients are mixed thoroughly and begin to boil
2. Turn the heat off. Pour the sauce into a bowl and allow to cool to room temperature. Pour into a glass jar and refrigerate until needed.

Lot Yau

Hot Oil

Commercial hot oil is sold in Chinese and Asian grocery stores under many names, including Hunan hot oil. I prefer making my own. Its strength is greater.

¹/₂ cup dried hot red pepper flakes
³/₄ cup sesame oil
³/₄ cup peanut oil

Makes 1¹/₂ cups

1. Place all ingredients in a large jar and mix well.
2. Close the jar tightly and place in a cool, dry place for 1 week, to allow the ingredients to blend. The oil will then be ready for use. It will keep indefinitely, refrigerated.

Vinegar Soy Sauce

See Cho Yau

Although this sauce may be made in advance, I prefer to make it as needed, so that it will be at full strength.

> 1 tablespoon dark soy sauce
> 1 tablespoon light soy sauce
> 1 ½ tablespoons white vinegar
> 1 tablespoon Hot Oil (page 37)
> 1 tablespoon finely sliced scallions, white and green portions
> ¼ cup Chicken Broth (page 33)

Makes ¾ cup

1. Combine all ingredients in a small bowl. Mix well. Allow the mixture to marinate for 30 minutes, then place in small soy sauce dishes for serving.

Ginger Soy Sauce

Geung Chung Yau

To ensure the best flavor, I prefer to make this as needed, instead of ahead of time.

> 1 teaspoon sugar
> 1 tablespoon dark soy sauce
> 1 tablespoon light soy sauce
> 1 teaspoon Scallion Oil (page 36)
> 3 tablespoons Chicken Broth (page 33)
> ½ tablespoon sesame oil
> 1 ½ tablespoons shredded fresh gingerroot
> 1 ½ tablespoons white portion of scallion, sliced thinly into ½-inch lengths
> A generous pinch of white pepper

Makes about ½ cup

1. Combine all ingredients in a small bowl. Mix well. Allow to stand for ½ hour, then serve in soy sauce dishes.

Seun Yau

Garlic Oil

This oil imparts a wonderful aroma to foods being cooked and to salads—both the oil and the sliced garlic. It is a fine addition to any soup, to which it should be added and stirred in just before serving. And its taste makes it a perfect dip. This is an oil I developed for my kitchen.

> **1 ¼ cups peanut oil**
> **1 ⅓ cups garlic (4 bulbs), peeled, thinly sliced**

Makes 1⅔ cups

1. Heat wok over high heat for 30 seconds. Add the peanut oil and the garlic and stir. Lower heat to medium and bring to a boil. Lower heat to low and allow to cook for 10 minutes or until the garlic turns light brown.

2. Turn off heat and allow to cool sufficiently to place in a glass jar. This will keep, in a closed jar, for about 4 weeks at room temperature, or indefinitely if refrigerated.

Seun See Yau

Garlic Pepper Sauce

The basic recipe for this sauce is claimed by Szechuan, Hunan, and Beijing, as well as Shanghai. Wherever it originated, it is a fine and pungent sauce, and I have improved upon it even more. The pepper flakes used are found at the bottom of my Hot Oil.

- 2 tablespoons light soy sauce
- 2 tablespoons dark soy sauce
- $^3/_4$ teaspoon soaked hot pepper flakes (see Hot Oil, page 37)
- 1 teaspoon sesame oil
- 1 tablespoon white vinegar
- 2 teaspoons Shao-Hsing wine or sherry
- 2 $^1/_2$ teaspoons sugar
- 1 tablespoon minced garlic
- 2 tablespoons scallions, green portion, minced
- 1 $^1/_2$ tablespoons minced red sweet pepper
- $^1/_2$ cup Chicken Broth (page 33)

Makes about 1 cup

1. Mix all ingredients. Allow to rest, in order to blend, for 1 hour before using.

Note: This sauce will keep, refrigerated, in a closed jar, for about 10 days.

Gai Lot

Hot Mustard

This is simply made by mixing equal amounts of mustard powder and cold tap water. Some prefer replacing the tap water with white distilled vinegar. There are many hot mustards on the market, but I prefer the English-made Colman's Mustard, Double Superfine Compound. It must be dried mustard, not the Colman's prepared mustard that comes in jars.

For a normal amount to accompany dim sum, you will use about 2 to 3 teaspoons of mustard powder to a similar amount of water (or vinegar).

In dim sum restaurants, soy sauce dishes are often filled half with mixed mustard, half with Chinese chili paste, which comes in jars. Mustard can, however, be served alone. Chili paste can also be served alone. If your tastes run to chili and the paste is unavailable, Tabasco sauce is an admirable substitute. Your taste for chilies, however, can easily be satisfied. Asian groceries have chili sauces or pastes, in jars and bottles, from China, Thailand, Hong Kong, and Indonesia. And the number of bottled chili sauces in addition to Tabasco is seemingly endless.

Curry Sauce

Gah Lei Jop

I developed this sauce, with its antecedents in India and Singapore, for my younger son, who would not eat shrimp unless they were accompanied by a curry sauce. Now the whole family has been converted.

1   cup Chicken Broth (page 33)
2 ½   teaspoons curry powder (Madras brand preferred)
1 ½   tablespoons tapioca flour mixed with 1 ½ tablespoons cold water

Makes about 1 cup

1. Place the chicken broth in a saucepan. Stir in the curry powder until it dissolves. Turn on the heat to medium and bring to a boil. Stir the tapioca flour–water mixture, then pour into saucepan. Quickly stir and mix and bring back to a boil. Turn off heat. Place in preheated sauce boat and serve.

Note: If you prefer your curry hotter, add ¼ teaspoon of cayenne pepper powder to the broth when you add the curry powder.

Seun Tim Jeung

Sweet and Sour Sauce

This pungent sauce is nearly identical to the sauce I make for that classic dish, sweet and sour pork. Although it does not contain either the vegetables or the fruit that are in that sauce, its taste remains quite direct.

$^1/_4$ cup sugar
$^1/_4$ cup white vinegar
$^1/_2$ cup cold water
$^1/_4$ teaspoon dark soy sauce
$^1/_4$ cup tomato sauce
$^1/_8$ teaspoon salt
3 $^1/_2$ teaspoons tapioca flour mixed with 3$^1/_2$ tea-
        spoons cold water

Makes about 1 cup

1. In a saucepan place all ingredients except tapioca flour–water mixture. Stir, making certain the salt and sugar dissolve and the mixture is well blended. Over medium heat bring to a boil, stirring several times. Stir the tapioca flour–water mixture, then pour into saucepan. Quickly stir well and allow to come to a boil. Turn off heat. Transfer to a preheated sauce boat and serve.

Red Oil

Hung Yau

This is an oil that is favored by the chefs of Szechuan. It is used both within recipes or as an accompaniment.

³/₄ **cup peanut oil**

3 **tablespoons cayenne pepper powder (Make certain you buy cayenne that is bright orange-red in color, which denotes fresh-ness. Old cayenne is dull in color.)**

Makes ¹/₂ cup oil, plus about ¹/₄ cup of cayenne, which settles on the bottom of the jar

1. Heat wok over high heat for 30 seconds. Add peanut oil and lower heat to low. Add the cayenne and stir well to mix. With heat still on low, allow the mixture to cook until you see wisps of smoke rising from the wok. Stir occasionally during the cooking so that the cayenne does not stick to the bottom of the wok, clot, and burn. It will not dissolve.

2. Turn off heat. Allow the mixture to cool sufficiently to place in a glass jar.

Note: This will keep 4 weeks at room temperature, or indefinitely when refrigerated. The jar must be closed.

Geung See
So Jop

Vinegar Ginger Dip

This is a traditional Shanghai accompaniment. It is usually served in small soy sauce dishes with Soup Buns or Soup Dumplings. However, it can be eaten with Potstickers and with Shanghai Street Dumplings as well.

1	tablespoon Chinkiang vinegar (or sherry wine vinegar)
6	tablespoons cold water
1 1/2	tablespoons dark soy sauce
1	teaspoon sugar
3	tablespoons shredded ginger

Makes 1/2 cup

1. Mix vinegar, water, soy sauce, and sugar well, until sugar dissolves. Add ginger. Allow to stand for 1 hour before serving.

Chapter 3

Doughs for Dumplings

The many doughs of dim sum and their changing consistencies and properties comprise perhaps the most important and intriguing aspect of dim sum dumpling cookery. Most dim sum are dumplings, buns, or breads based on white dough. While the majority are made from wheat flour, some are made from glutinous rice flower, and a very few are made from rice flour. All flours are called *fun,* or powder, by the Chinese, so that wheat flour is *mien fun*, a high-gluten wheat flour or noodle flour is *gun mien fun*, glutinous rice flour is *nor mai fun*, and rice flour is *jim mai fun*.

For those who have a passion, small or large, for baking, for making, kneading, or molding dough, these doughs will have a special pleasure. Bread makers relate how close they feel to their dough and breads; this is not at all a misplaced emotion. So it is with these several doughs. For many of the dim sum recipes in this book, ready-made wrappers can be bought, and wonderful dumplings can be fashioned from them, to be sure. These are so noted in the course of this book. But other dim sum recipes require the making of dough, a creative process I know you will absolutely enjoy.

All of the flours and starches used in the preparation of these doughs are pure white. This aspect is most pleasing to the Chinese, for whom the appearance of their dim sum is as important as the taste. For them, dim sum must be white, and the whiter the flour the whiter the steamed or baked dough will be.

White flour is simply the end product of the milling process. It is the most commonly used flour and comes from the wheat kernel, which also includes the coarse outer layer called bran, the oily germ, and the starchy core called the endosperm. The bran and germ contain most of the wheat's vitamins and minerals, but because they spoil rather quickly and make for a rough-textured product, these are discarded in the milling of fine white flour. Since this flour contains only endosperm, which has few vitamins or minerals, it is "enriched" with additions of iron, thiamin, riboflavin, and niacin.

The gluten portion of flour—actually its protein component—is what gives elasticity to dough. The more gluten in the flour, the more elastic the dough and the greater its strength. Gluten is often added to a white flour too, in the form of gluten flour. This is manufactured by preparing a dough from the regular wheat flour, washing away its starch-laden portion, drying what is left, and then grinding it finely. The protein content of white flour is usually about 10 percent; with gluten flour added, this rises to about 12 percent. But more important, the addition of gluten makes regular white flour more elastic.

In general, flour is milled for dim sum and the dumpling makers and is sold to restaurants in one-hundred-pound bags. Obviously it cannot be expected that you or I will buy flour in such quantities, so I have experimented meticulously with flours readily available on market shelves, in quantities as small as two-pound sacks.

The following list explains some of the various descriptions found on flour bag labels.

> All-Purpose Flour: Flour composed of half hard wheat with gluten for tensile strength, and half soft wheat that is better quality flour.
>
> Enriched Flour: Flour with added nutrition.
>
> Bread Flour: Usually flour with high-gluten content.
>
> Bromide Flour: A combination of wheat flour and malted barley flour.
>
> Short Patent: White flour, often made whiter by gas.
>
> Standard Patent: Less white.

For purposes of dim sum cookery, the important characteristics of flour are that it is white, that it has a high proportion of gluten, and that it contains hard wheat for strength. I have already listed the wheat flours that have proved to be the most dependable under all cooking and climate conditions, those I prefer to use in order to make the finest of each particular dumpling. I have named these flours where indicated in the recipes.

Other flours or powders are sometimes added to white flour dough. The most common are tapioca powder (ground from the root of the cassava) and glutinous rice powder (ground from dry glutinous rice). Both add tensile strength to their dough.

A few of these dim sum—*Har Gau* and its close relatives are the first example—require that you make a dough. With most of the dumplings however, they can be made either with the dough specified or with dumpling wrappers or skins already made available in markets. In all cases I have indicated these alternatives.

The pleasure lies in the dough. Whether you work your own, or use those prepared, I trust that you will enjoy the processes of dim sum.

The Wheat Starch–Tapioca Flour dough recipe is a tradition of many centuries. To this day, in dim sum restaurants and teahouses, these dumplings are made the way they have always been made, with fresh rolled-out dough. I compare this to any tradition of the French kitchen of Escoffier, who described ways of cooking that have become classics.

You will note that no alternative ready-made wrappings are offered in place of this dough. That is because there are no alternatives. You may, of course, put the fillings of these dim sum into ready-made wrappings, but they cannot be steamed. If you attempt to steam them, the wrappings become tough and rubbery. They must be boiled. Which of course will give you some sort of a dumpling, but not the fine traditional *Har Gau* and its relations.

Wheat Starch-Tapioca Flour Dough

This dough is a favorite of the master dim sum chefs, the dai see fu, of the Chinese kitchen, because it can be shaped and sculpted. It is perhaps the most traditional of dumpling dough, which is used for a variety of dim sum preparations and is not at all difficult to form. The small, individual pieces of the dough, used to fashion the dumplings are called pei, *or "skins," in the Chinese kitchen.*

> 1 **cup wheat starch**
> 1/2 **cup tapioca flour**
> 1/4 **teaspoon salt (optional)**
> 1 **cup boiling water**
> 1 1/2 **tablespoons peanut oil**

To Form the Dough

1. In a bowl place the wheat starch, the tapioca flour, and the salt. Mix well. Pour in boiling water and mix quickly. Add peanut oil and continue to mix. I find mixing is best with a pair of chopsticks or a wooden spoon. The consistency should resemble a biscuit mix, dry and slightly crumbly. Mix until the dough, while still heated, is sufficiently cool to the touch, and can be kneaded.

2. Knead with your hand in the bowl until a smooth mass of dough is formed. Remove from bowl, knead a few times, then cut the dough in half and place both halves in a plastic bag. Allow to cool and to sit for at least 30 minutes before working with it.

To Form the Skins

1. Before working with the dough, oil the work surface. Soak a paper towel in peanut oil and repeatedly rub across the blade of a Chinese cleaver across the folded towel so that the blade is slightly oiled.

2. Roll each half of the dough into a sausage-shaped length. The lengths will vary with the sizes of the dumplings made, as you will see, but each length will be cut into 1-inch segments. Each

segment will be rolled into a small ball, then pressed down with the palm of the hand, then finally pressed flat with the broad side of the Chinese cleaver to create round dumpling skins. (These rounds will vary in size as well, with dumplings made, but the technique employed is identical.)

Note: When working with the dough half, use one at a time and keep the other in the plastic bag. For each of the following dumplings that use this skin, you should make five skins at a time. The remaining pieces should be kept under plastic wrap. Always do your dumplings in multiples of five. This ensures the dough will remain moist and pliable.

Note: When making each individual skin, a tortilla press rubbed with peanut oil may be used. The skin produced will be thicker, however. I prefer using the cleaver blade, the classic way of the dim sum chefs.

蝦餃

Har Gau

Shrimp Dumplings

Har Gau is the most famous dim sum in China, and if one is to judge by the number consumed at dim sum restaurants everywhere, perhaps in the world. It is light and delicate and favored by all. Chinese children regard Har Gau *with the same reverence that American children give to hamburgers.*

½ **pound shrimp, shelled, deveined, washed,**
      dried, diced
½ **teaspoon salt**
1½ **teaspoons sugar**
1 **egg white, jumbo size, beaten**
1½ **tablespoons tapioca flour**
2 **teaspoons oyster sauce**
1½ **teaspoons sesame oil**
   Pinch of white pepper
¼ **cup water chestnuts, diced**
⅓ **cup white portion of scallions, finely**
      chopped
¼ **cup bamboo shoots, diced**
1 **Wheat Starch–Tapioca Flour Dough recipe**
      (page 50)

Makes 30 dumplings

1. Place shrimp in a large bowl. Add salt, sugar, egg white, tapioca flour, oyster sauce, sesame oil, and white pepper and mix together. Add water chestnuts, scallions, and bamboo shoots and combine thoroughly and evenly. Remove the mixture from the bowl, place it in a shallow dish, and refrigerate uncovered for 4 hours, or overnight, covered.

2. With Wheat Starch–Tapioca Flour Dough, using the techniques as described, make two sausage-shaped lengths of dough, 15 inches each. Cut each length into 15 one-inch segments. Make dumpling skins 3 inches in diameter. Form 5 at a time, keeping dough not being used under plastic wrap.

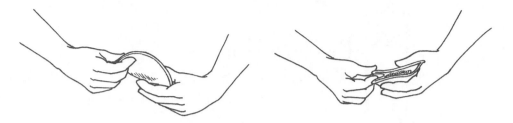

3. Form the dumplings: Place 1½ teaspoons of shrimp filling into the center of each skin, then fold the skin in half, forming a crescent or half-moon shape.

4. Hold the dumpling securely in your left hand, then begin to form pleats with the fingers of your right hand along the curve of the crescent. Continue to form small pleats until the dumpling is completely closed. Press the top pleated edge of the dumpling between your thumb and index fingers to seal it tightly. Tap the sealed edge lightly with your knuckle to give the dumpling its final shape. Repeat until all dumplings are done. (As your proficiency increases, increase the filling to 2 teaspoons.)

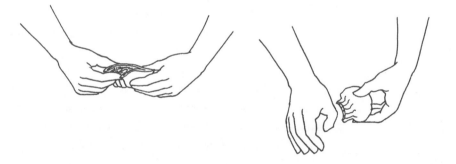

5. Steam the dumplings for 7 minutes and serve immediately.

Serving Suggestion: I prefer eating *Har Gau* without a sauce or dip, but try them with a bit of Hot Mustard (page 41), or with a mix of the mustard with Chinese chili paste.

Note: *Har Gau* may be frozen for future use. They will keep at least 3 months when piled neatly and wrapped in a double layer of plastic wrap and then in foil. To reheat, defrost, then steam for 3 to 5 minutes.

*Fung Ngan
Gau*

Phoenix Eyes

The phoenix is the traditional symbol of the bride or of the woman of nobility, and these dumplings are shaped to look like a woman's eyes.

³/₄ **pound shrimp, shelled, deveined, washed, dried, diced**

¹/₂ **teaspoon salt, to taste**

1 **egg white, large, beaten**

2¹/₂ **tablespoons tapioca flour**

1¹/₂ **teaspoons sugar**

1 **teaspoon sesame oil**

1 **tablespoon oyster sauce**

Pinch of white pepper

¹/₄ **cup white portions of scallions, finely sliced**

1 **tablespoon Garlic Oil (page 39)**

2 **teaspoons white wine**

1 **Wheat Starch–Tapioca Flour Dough recipe (page 50)**

Makes 26 dumplings

1. Make the filling: place shrimp in a bowl. Add salt, egg white, tapioca flour, sugar, sesame oil, oyster sauce, white pepper, scallions, garlic oil, and wine and blend thoroughly and evenly 5 to 7 minutes. Refrigerate uncovered 4 hours or overnight, covered.

2. With Wheat Starch–Tapioca Flour Dough, using the techniques as described, make 2 sausage-shaped lengths of dough, each 13 inches long. Cut each length into 1-inch segments. Make dumpling skins 3¹/₂ inches in diameter. Form 5 at a time, keeping dough not being used under plastic wrap.

3. Form the dumplings: Place 1 tablespoon of filling in center of each skin. Fold the skin in half to form a crescent shape. With your index fingers, create a vertical pleat on each of the dumpling's sides. Press and seal the side edges of the dumpling to form the phoenix eye shape, with ends of dumpling

squeezed together and not divided. Repeat until all dumplings are made. (As your proficiency increases you may increase the filling to 4 teaspoons.)

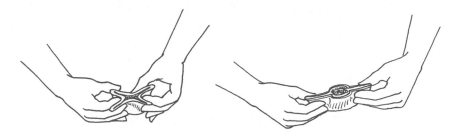

4.   Steam for 7 minutes and serve immediately.

Serving Suggestion: As with *Har Gau,* I prefer eating Phoenix Eyes without accompaniment. But some people prefer eating them with the same sauces as *Har Gau,* either with a bit of Hot Mustard (page 41) or with a mix of the mustard and Chinese chili paste.

Note: *Fung Ngan Gau* may be frozen and will keep about 3 months. To freeze, wrap in a couple of layers of plastic wrap and then in foil. To reheat, defrost thoroughly and steam for 3 to 5 minutes.

Fun Guor

Rice Noodle Fruit

These are oddly named, and though I am often asked the origin of "rice noodle fruit," I must reply that I do not know it. It is sufficient to say that is what it is called by the dim sum masters. Perhaps it might be because the half-moon shape looks like a slice of apple or an orange wedge.

Sauce Ingredients

- $1/4$ teaspoon salt
- $1^1/2$ teaspoons sugar
- 1 teaspoon sesame oil
- 1 teaspoon light soy sauce
- $2^1/2$ tablespoons tapioca flour
- $1^1/2$ tablespoons oyster sauce
- Pinch of white pepper
- $1/2$ cup Chicken Broth (page 33) or chicken soup

To Continue Recipe

- 2 tablespoons finely chopped fresh coriander
- 1 Wheat Starch–Tapioca Flour Dough recipe (page 50)

To Finish the Dish

- 1 tablespoon peanut oil
- $1/2$ pound coarsely ground pork, to which $3/4$ teaspoon of tapioca flour is added, and mixed well
- 3 ounces shrimp, shelled, deveined, washed, dried, diced
- 2–3 Chinese black mushrooms, soaked to soften, diced into $1/8$-inch pieces ($1/4$ cup)
- $1/2$ cup winter bamboo shoots, diced into $1/8$-inch pieces
- 1 tablespoon white wine

Makes 30 dumplings

1. Mix sauce ingredients. Reserve.
2. Heat wok over high heat for 30 seconds. Add peanut oil and

coat wok with spatula. When a wisp of white smoke appears add pork. Stir, then add shrimp, mushrooms, and bamboo shoots. Stir together well. Add wine and cook until pork darkens and shrimp turn pink, about 2 minutes.

3. Add the sauce to the wok. Cook until the sauce thickens and turns brown, then add coriander. Remove from wok, place in a shallow dish, and refrigerate, uncovered, overnight.

4. With Wheat Starch–Tapioca Flour Dough, using techniques described, roll dough into 2 sausage-shaped lengths, each 15 inches long. Cut each length into 15 one-inch segments. Make dumpling skins, 3 inches in diameter. Form 5 at a time, keeping dough not being used under plastic wrap.

5. Form the dumplings: Place 1 tablespoon of the filling in center of skin and fold into a half-moon shape. Squeeze curved edge to seal.

6. Steam 5 to 6 minutes. Serve immediately.

Serving Suggestion: I prefer not to have any sauce or dip with these rice noodle fruits. I enjoy the blended tastes of the pork and shrimp unadorned.

Note: *Fun Guor* may be frozen but will keep only about 4 weeks. Wrap in a double layer of plastic wrap, then in foil. To reheat, defrost thoroughly and steam 3 to 5 minutes.

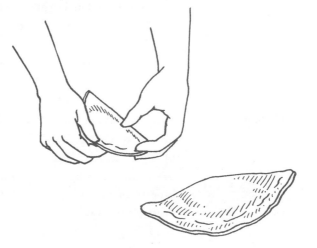

Jai Gau

Vegetarian Dumplings

The Chinese are a most practical people. Years ago, vegetarian dumplings were virtually unknown and strict vegetarians were few. Now, because more people are looking to vegetables for complete diets, I've included this and other vegetable dumplings.

2	cups peanut oil (to blanch vegetables)
$^1/_2$	cup snow peas, shredded
$^1/_2$	cup carrots, shredded
$^1/_2$	cup celery, shredded
$^1/_2$	cup bamboo shoots, shredded
2	fresh water chestnuts, shredded
5	Chinese black mushrooms, soaked to soften, shredded ($^1/_2$ cup)
$^1/_2$	tablespoon peanut oil

Sauce Ingredients

1	tablespoon oyster sauce
1	tablespoon dark soy sauce
$2^1/_2$	tablespoons tapioca flour
$^1/_2$	teaspoon salt
1	teaspoon sugar
$^1/_2$	teaspoon sesame oil
	Pinch white pepper
4	tablespoons cold water

To Continue Recipe

1	Wheat Starch–Tapioca Flour Dough recipe (page 50)

Makes 34 dumplings

1. Heat wok over high heat for 30 seconds. Add 2 cups of peanut oil and heat to 325°F to 350°F. Place vegetables in hot oil and blanch for 30 to 40 seconds. Remove vegetables from oil and drain them through a strainer. Set the vegetables aside. Combine the sauce ingredients and reserve.

2. Pour oil from wok and wipe clean with paper towel, then heat $^1/_2$ tablespoon of peanut oil in the wok until a wisp of white

smoke appears. Add the sauce and cook until it thickens and turns dark brown. Turn off heat. Add reserved vegetables to sauce and mix well until all vegetables are coated. Remove mixture from wok, place in a shallow dish, and refrigerate, uncovered, at least 4 hours or overnight.

3. With Wheat Starch–Tapioca Flour Dough, using techniques described, roll dough into 2 sausage-shaped lengths, each 17 inches long. Cut each into 17 one-inch segments. Make dumpling skins, 2¾ inches in diameter. Form 5 at a time, keeping dough not being used under plastic wrap.

4. Form the dumplings: Place 2 teaspoons of the vegetable filling in the center of the skin and fold into a half-moon shape. Squeeze curved edge to seal.

5. Steam for 5 minutes. Serve immediately.

Serving Suggestion: I recommend eating these dumplings with Hot Oil (page 37).

Note: Vegetarian dumplings cannot be frozen.

Chive Dumplings

Gau Choi Gau

This is a dumpling of the southern Cantonese people, the Chiu Chow. I have enjoyed these dumplings in Hong Kong so often that I brought the recipe home to my kitchen.

Sauce Ingredients

- ³/₄ teaspoon light soy sauce
- 1 teaspoon Shao-Hsing wine or sherry
- ³/₄ teaspoon sugar
- 1¹/₂ tablespoons oyster sauce
- 5 teaspoons cornstarch
  Pinch of white pepper
- 4 tablespoons Chicken Broth (page 33)

Pork Marinade

- 6 ounces lean pork, ground
- ¹/₂ teaspoon light soy sauce
- ³/₄ teaspoon sugar
- 1 teaspoon sesame oil
- 1¹/₂ teaspoons Shao-Hsing wine or sherry
- 1¹/₂ teaspoons oyster sauce
- 1¹/₂ teaspoons cornstarch
  Pinch of white pepper

To Continue Recipe

- 2 tablespoons Garlic Oil (page 39)
- ¹/₄ teaspoon salt
- 2 teaspoons ginger, minced
- ¹/₂ pound Chinese chives (garlic chives) washed, dried thoroughly, cut into ¹/₃-inch pieces
- 1 Wheat Starch–Tapioca Flour Dough recipe (page 50)

Makes 24 dumplings

1. Combine the sauce ingredients. Reserve. Combine the marinade ingredients and add the pork. Reserve.
2. Heat a wok over high heat for 30 seconds. Add garlic oil, salt, and ginger. Coat wok with spatula. When a wisp of white smoke

appears add chives. Stir and cook until chives turn bright green and their fragrance is released, about 1 minute. Add pork and marinade and mix thoroughly, about 1 minute. Make a well in the center of the mixture, stir the sauce, and pour in. Mix well; when sauce begins to thicken, turn off heat. Transfer to a shallow dish, allow to cool, then refrigerate for 4 hours, uncovered.

3. With Wheat Starch–Tapioca Flour Dough, using techniques described, roll dough into 2 sausage-shaped lengths, each 12 inches long. Cut each into 12 one-inch segments. Make dumpling skins 3½ inches in diameter. Form 5 at a time, keeping dough not being used under plastic wrap.

4. Form the dumplings: Place 1 tablespoon of the filling in the center of the skin. Gather the edges of the skin together to cover the filling and squeeze shut, making a round bundle. Twist the skin at the point of closure and break off the surplus dough. Place the dumpling, sealed side down, in a steamer. Repeat until all dumplings are made.

5. Steam for 7 minutes. Serve immediately.

Serving Suggestion: I prefer eating these dumplings without any dip or sauce.

Note: Chive dumplings should not be frozen.

Dau Miu Gau

Snow Pea Shoot Dumplings

This dumpling, or gau, is a modern adaptation of a traditional dim sum dumpling of Canton. It originated in Hong Kong, where chefs like to create variations on a theme, particularly when they can use fresh vegetables. This dumpling traditionally is made with pork or shrimp. I have made it with those very sweet snow pea shoots mixed with flavored shrimp, a kind of salute to tradition and to Hong Kong.

$^1/_2$ pound snow pea shoots, washed, dried, cut into $^1/_2$-inch pieces

4 cups cold water

$^1/_2$ teaspoon baking soda

$^1/_2$ teaspoon salt

$^1/_2$ pound shrimp, shelled, deveined, washed, dried, coarsely chopped

1 tablespoon young ginger, minced, or 1$^1/_2$ teaspoons regular ginger

1$^1/_2$ tablespoons oyster sauce

1 teaspoon light soy sauce

1 teaspoon Shao-Hsing wine or sherry

$^1/_4$ teaspoon salt

1$^1/_2$ teaspoons sugar

2 teaspoons sesame oil

2 tablespoons cornstarch

Pinch of white pepper

1 Wheat Starch–Tapioca Flour Dough recipe (page 50)

Makes 24 dumplings

1. Water blanch the snow pea shoots: In a large pot place cold water, baking soda, and salt. Bring to a boil. Add snow pea shoots. Make certain they are submerged, stir, and allow water to return to a boil. Turn off heat. Run cold water into pot. Drain. Repeat. Drain thoroughly. Reserve.

2. Make the filling: In a large bowl place the snow pea shoots, the

shrimp, and all other ingredients except the dough. Mix thoroughly until well blended. Place in a shallow dish, and refrigerate for 4 hours, uncovered.

3. With Wheat Starch–Tapioca Flour Dough, using techniques described, roll dough into 2 sausage-shaped lengths, each 12 inches long. Cut each into 12 one-inch segments. Make dumpling skins 3½ inches in diameter. Form 5 at a time, keeping dough not being used under plastic wrap.

4. Form the dumplings: Place 1 tablespoon of the filling in the center of the skin. Gather the edges of the skin together to cover the filling and squeeze shut, making a round bundle. Twist the skin at the point of closure and break off the surplus dough. Place the dumpling, the sealed side down, in a steamer. Repeat until all dumplings are made.

5. Steam for 7 minutes. Serve immediately.

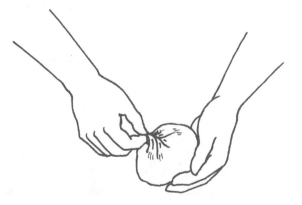

Serving Suggestion: I prefer eating these dumplings without any dip or sauce.

Note: Snow Pea Shoot Dumplings should not be frozen.

Wheat Flour Dough

This dough is simple and basic and is that used most widely in the dim sum kitchen. Squares of it may be bought in Chinese markets, even occasionally in supermarkets. I suggest that you do buy them because they are usually rolled quite thin, thinner perhaps than you could roll them at home. If, however, you do not have access to these ready-made dumpling skins, here is an easy recipe.

1¼ **cups flour, Pillsbury Best All-Purpose, enriched, bleached preferred**

½ **teaspoon baking soda**

2 **extra-large eggs**

2 **tablespoons water**

⅓ **cup cornstarch, for dusting**

Makes 36 skins

1. Combine the flour and baking soda and place the mixture on a work surface. Make a well in the center and add the eggs. Work the dough with your fingers until all of the egg has been absorbed. Slowly dribble in the water, mixing as you do, until the dough is thoroughly mixed. Use a dough scraper to pick up excess dough. Begin to knead.

2. Knead the dough for 5 minutes or until it becomes elastic. Set aside, covered with a damp cloth, for 4 hours.

3. When the dough is ready, dust the work surface with cornstarch. Roll out the dough with a rolling pin until you have a sheet that is ¼ inch thick. Pick up the sheet and dust the work surface again with cornstarch. Continue rolling out the dough until it reaches an overall thickness of ⅛ inch.

4. Roll up the dough around a long piece of broom handle or dowel. Dust the work surface again. Roll the dough out with the pin, as thinly as possible, then roll the dough around the broom handle again. (You must pick up the dough by rolling it around the broom handle, otherwise it will tear.)

5. Dust the work surface again. Unroll the sheet onto the surface and with the rolling pin roll out to about 21 inches square.

6. Before cutting, be certain to dust the work surface again with cornstarch. Using the edge of a dough scraper to cut, and the edge of a ruler to measure and guide, cut out $3\frac{1}{2}$-inch squares from the sheet. As you stack them after cutting, sprinkle each with cornstarch to prevent sticking.

Note: This dough should be made the night before using. The skins will be more elastic if stored overnight in the refrigerator after being wrapped in plastic wrap.

Different recipes using this dough require different numbers of skins. Extra skins may be frozen for 2 months.

The ready-made dough squares can be bought as "won ton" skins. They come in 1-pound packages, usually 90 to 100 skins to the pound, and in varying thickness. I prefer the thinner ones, so I recommend that you buy the skins, since commercial makers can make them thinner than you will be able to. Here is a guide for buying these skins:

"Won ton skins" come square, about $3\frac{1}{4}$ inches on a side. These may also be labeled "won ton wrappers."

"Water dumpling skins" are round, from $3\frac{1}{4}$ to $3\frac{1}{2}$ inches in diameter. These may also be labeled "Hong Kong style."

"Dumpling skins" are usually round.

These are all the same, so look for those labels in the refrigerated compartments of Chinese or Asian groceries. You might even see a label for "suey gow." This is phonetic Cantonese for "water dumpling" skins.

There are many brands; all are about equal. Use them when they are bought. Any left over may be frozen. They will keep 2 months, double-wrapped in plastic wrap, then in foil. **To use:** If frozen, allow them to defrost and come to room temperature. As you work, treat them as if you were working with a dough you had made—cover those not being used with a damp cloth to preserve their softness and flexibility.

Siu Mai

Cook and Sell Dumplings

These dim sum bear the delightful description, "Cook and Sell," simply because they are shaped like tiny cooking kettles filled with food. And because they are so tasty and so pretty they are never left unsold.

6   Chinese black mushrooms, soaked for 30 minutes in hot water, rinsed, dried, stems discarded, caps diced into $1/4$-inch pieces
$1/2$ pound coarsely ground pork
$1/4$ pound shrimp, shelled, deveined, washed, dried, diced into $1/4$-inch pieces
$1/2$ teaspoon salt
$1 1/4$ teaspoons sugar
1   tablespoon peanut oil
1   tablespoon oyster sauce
1   tablespoon cornstarch
1   teaspoon sesame oil
    Pinch of white pepper
1   Wheat Flour Dough recipe (page 64) or 22 commercial skins

Makes 22 dumplings

1. In a large bowl combine all ingredients (except skins) and mix until the consistency is smooth and even. Refrigerate for 4 hours, uncovered.

2. Using kitchen shears or a round cookie cutter cut skins into rounds $2 1/2$ inches in diameter.

3. Into the middle of each skin place 4 teaspoons of filling. Hold the filling in place with the blade of a small rounded knife in one hand, and holding the dumpling in the other hand, gradually turn knife and dumpling slowly in the same direction, so dumpling forms a basket shape.

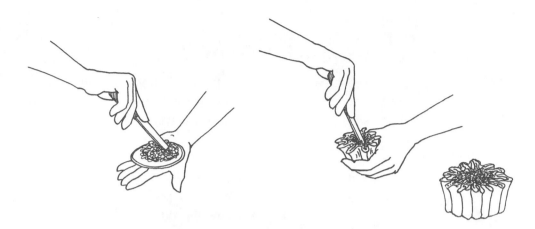

4. Remove the knife, pack down, and smooth the filling on top of
    dumpling. Squeeze the dumpling lightly to create a "neck" so
    that the dumpling and filling will remain intact during the steam-
    ing process. Tap dumpling lightly on the work surface to flat-
    ten the bottom so that it will stand upright in the steamer.

5. Steam for 7 minutes. Serve immediately.

Serving Suggestion: I prefer to eat this dumpling without
accompaniment. However I know that a mixture of Hot Mustard (page 41) and Chinese chili paste will complement it nicely.

Note: *Siu Mai* can be frozen after steaming. They will keep 2 to
3 months, wrapped in plastic wrap and then in foil. To reheat,
defrost thoroughly and steam 3 to 5 minutes.

Gah Lei Siu Mai

Curried *Siu Mai*

This is my variation of the theme of a traditional dim sum. I add curry to the basic recipe, and a whole new dumpling is created. Rarely, if ever, will you find this in a dim sum restaurant or teahouse. So enjoy it at home.

Curry Paste Ingredients

2 teaspoons peanut oil

1 teaspoon minced ginger

1 teaspoon minced garlic

2 tablespoons minced fresh coriander

2$\frac{1}{2}$ teaspoons curry powder mixed with 2$\frac{1}{2}$ teaspoons cold water

3 tablespoons cold water

1 beef bouillon cube

Filling Ingredients

$\frac{1}{2}$ pound ground pork, lean

$\frac{1}{4}$ pound shrimp, shelled, deveined, washed, dried, diced

3 fresh water chestnuts, peeled, cut into $\frac{1}{8}$-inch dice ($\frac{1}{3}$ cup)

3 scallions, white portions, finely sliced ($\frac{1}{3}$ cup)

1$\frac{3}{4}$ teaspoons sugar

$\frac{1}{4}$ teaspoon salt

1 teaspoon sesame oil

1$\frac{1}{2}$ tablespoons oyster sauce

Pinch white pepper

1$\frac{1}{2}$ tablespoons cornstarch

1 teaspoon light soy sauce

1 Wheat Flour Dough recipe (page 64) or 24 commercial skins

1 scallion, green portion, finely sliced, for garnish (2 tablespoons)

Makes 24 dumplings

1. Make curry paste: In a small pot, over high heat, heat the peanut oil. When a wisp of white smoke appears, add the minced ginger and garlic. Stir and cook for 20 seconds. Add the coriander, stir, and mix well. When garlic turns light brown, add the curry mixture. Stir well and cook for 30 seconds or until the aroma is released. Add the 3 tablespoons of cold water, stir. Add beef bouillon cube, making certain the cube dissolves. Stir until paste is smooth and blended. Cover pot, lower heat, and simmer 10 minutes. Stir occasionally so curry does not burn. Turn off heat. Reserve.

2. Make the filling: Combine pork, shrimp, filling ingredients, and curry paste in a bowl. Mix thoroughly until well blended. Remove to a shallow dish and refrigerate for 4 hours, uncovered.

3. Make dumplings: With kitchen shears or a cookie cutter cut each skin into a round 2½ inches in diameter. Into the middle of each skin place 1 tablespoon of filling. Follow directions exactly as given in steps 3 and 4 of *Siu Mai* (pages 66–67).

4. Before steaming sprinkle green portions of scallions over the dumplings. Steam for 7 minutes. Serve immediately.

Serving Suggestion: I prefer not to serve these with any accompaniment because of the curry taste; yet a couple of drops of Red Oil (page 44) on each dumpling will heighten their taste.

Note: *Gah Lei Siu Mai* can be frozen after steaming. They will keep 2 to 3 months, wrapped in plastic wrap, then in foil. To reheat, defrost thoroughly and steam 3 to 5 minutes.

Veal Siu Mai

Ngau Jai Yuk
Siu Mai

The words ngau jai yuk *translate as "meat of the suckling cow." Veal is rare, even today, in many parts of China, but in Hong Kong it is eaten widely. I enjoy making dim sum with veal because the flavor of the meat blends quite well with traditional ingredients. This, then, is a new "Cook and Sell."*

10	ounces lean ground veal
$^1/_3$	cup fresh water chestnuts, cut into $^1/_8$-inch dice
$^1/_3$	cup bamboo shoots, cut into $^1/_8$-inch dice
$^1/_4$	cup scallions, white portion, finely sliced
1	tablespoon minced ginger
1	tablespoon Shao-Hsing wine or sherry
$^1/_4$	teaspoon salt
$1^1/_2$	teaspoons sugar
1	teaspoon double dark soy sauce
$1^1/_2$	tablespoons oyster sauce
$1^1/_2$	tablespoons Garlic Oil (page 39)
$1^1/_2$	tablespoons cornstarch
1	teaspoon sesame oil
	Pinch white pepper
1	extra-large egg white, beaten
1	Wheat Flour Dough recipe (page 64) or 24 commercial skins

Makes 24 dumplings

1. Make the filling: Combine the veal with all other ingredients (except the skins) and mix thoroughly to blend well. Refrigerate in a shallow dish, uncovered, for 4 hours.
2. Make the dumplings: With kitchen shears or a cookie cutter cut each skin into a round 2½ inches in diameter. Place one tablespoon of filling in the center of the skin. Follow directions exactly as given in steps 3 and 4 of *Siu Mai* (pages 66–67).
3. Steam dumplings 5 to 6 minutes. Remove from steamer and serve immediately.

Serving Suggestion: I prefer to serve these dumplings with Ginger Soy Sauce (page 38) as a dip.

Note: *Ngau Jai Yuk* can be frozen after steaming. They will keep 2 to 3 months, wrapped in plastic wrap, then in foil. To reheat, defrost thoroughly and steam 3 to 5 minutes.

Far Siu Mai

Flower Dumplings

The traditional shape of Siu Mai reminds some people of baskets; to others these are like tulips just opening. Often they are called "flower dumplings." Here is a flower filled with chicken and vegetables, a spring dumpling.

$1/2$ **pound chicken breast, ground**
$1/4$ **cup jícama, finely diced**
$1/4$ **cup carrot, finely diced**
$1/3$ **cup scallions, finely sliced**
$3/4$ **teaspoon grated ginger**
1 **egg white, lightly beaten**
$1^1/2$ **tablespoons peanut oil**
$1^1/2$ **teaspoons sesame oil**
1 **teaspoon Shao-Hsing wine or sherry**
1 **teaspoon light soy sauce**
$3/4$ **teaspoon salt**
$1^3/4$ **teaspoons sugar**
2 **tablespoons cornstarch**
  Pinch of white pepper
1 **Wheat Flour Dough recipe (page 64) or 24 commercial skins**

Makes 24 dumplings

1. In a large bowl combine the chicken and all other ingredients (except skins) and mix thoroughly to blend well. Remove to a shallow dish and refrigerate for 4 hours, uncovered.

2. Make the dumplings: Cut each skin into a round 2³/₄ inches in diameter. Place 1 tablespoon of filling in the center of the skin. Follow directions exactly as given in steps 3 and 4 of *Siu Mai* (pages 66–67).

3. Steam dumplings 8 to 10 minutes. Remove from steamer and serve immediately.

Serving Suggestion: I suggest serving these with Sweet Scallion Sauce (page 37) as a dip.

Note: Flower Dumplings can be frozen after steaming. They will keep 6 to 8 weeks, wrapped in plastic wrap, then in foil. To reheat, defrost thoroughly and steam 3 to 5 minutes.

Nor Mai Siu Mai

Glutinous Rice *Siu Mai*

This is another adaptation of a traditional siu mai, *a true dim sum dumpling of dough with a filling of seasoned glutinous rice. In China, stir-fried glutinous rice is a winter custom. I have taken all of the ingredients for this winter dish and created a dim sum that requires no frying at all. The combination of the flavored rice and the steamed dough is irresistible.*

1	cup glutinous rice
1	cup water
2	Chinese sausages (see note)
¹/₂	tablespoon dried shrimp, soaked in hot water 30 minutes, diced
¹/₄	teaspoon salt
1	teaspoon sugar
1¹/₄	teaspoons light soy sauce
¹/₂	teaspoon dark soy sauce
1	tablespoon oyster sauce

1 scallion, ends discarded, finely sliced
2 teaspoons Garlic Oil (page 39)
2 tablespoons finely chopped fresh coriander
1 Wheat Flour dough recipe (page 64) or
    24 commercial skins
3 tablespoons green portion of scallions,
    finely sliced, to garnish

Makes 24 dumplings

1. Wash and rinse the glutinous rice 3 times and drain. In a 9-inch cake pan, place the rice and add 1 cup water. Lay the 2 sausages on top of the rice. Place cake pan in a bamboo steamer and cover. Pour 6 cups of water into a wok and over high heat bring to a boil. Place the steamer in the wok above the water and steam for 30 minutes or until the rice becomes translucent. Remove from steamer. Allow rice to cool to the touch. Cut the sausage into ¼-inch dice.

2. Make the filling: Place rice in a large bowl. Add diced sausages and all other ingredients (except the skins and sliced scallions for garnish). Mix thoroughly until well blended.

3. Make the dumplings: With kitchen shears or a cookie cutter cut skins into rounds 2½ inches in diameter. Place 1 tablespoon of filling in center of each round. Follow directions exactly as given in steps 3 and 4 of *Siu Mai* (pages 66–67).

4. Steam for 7 minutes. Remove from steamer and serve immediately.

Serving Suggestion: I prefer not to have a sauce or dip with these dumplings. My husband likes Sweet Scallion Sauce (page 37).

Note: These dumplings cannot be frozen. The rice will not retain its gluten or its texture, and the dumpling will be formless.

Note: If you cannot find Chinese sausages, a breakfast-type sausage can be used instead. The texture will be the same, but the taste will be quite different.

Water Dumplings

Soi Gau

The Chinese very aptly call these "water dumplings" because they are cooked, either completely or partially, in boiling water. In the traditional teahouse the cooking process is often completed by steaming them in small, individual serving steamers, after boiling. At home, however, these are simply boiled.

¹/₂ pound fresh ground pork

2 ounces shrimp, shelled, deveined, washed, dried, diced

3 tablespoons bamboo shoots, cut into ¹/₈-inch dice

3 tablespoons fresh water chestnuts, peeled, cut into ¹/₈-inch dice

¹/₄ cup white portion scallions, finely chopped

³/₄ teaspoon salt

1³/₄ teaspoons sesame oil

Pinch of white pepper

1 tablespoon tapioca flour

1 egg, beaten

1 Wheat Flour Dough recipe (page 64) or 24 commercial skins

To Boil Dumplings

2 quarts cold water

1 teaspoon salt

1 tablespoon peanut oil

Makes 24 dumplings

1. In a bowl combine the pork and all other ingredients except beaten egg, skins, and boiling ingredients. Blend evenly and thoroughly. Refrigerate in a shallow dish, uncovered, for 4 hours.

2. Make the dumplings: With kitchen shears or a cookie cutter cut skins into rounds 3 inches in diameter. Place 3 teaspoons of filling in center of a skin. With a butter knife, brush egg around the outer edge of skin. Fold skin into a half-moon shape

and press together along the curved edge tightly with thumb and forefinger to seal. Continue until all dumplings are made. (As your proficiency grows increase filling amount to 4 teaspoons.)

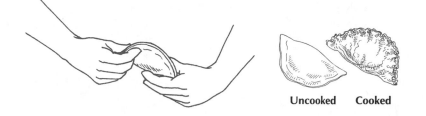

Uncooked   Cooked

3. Cook dumplings in 2 quarts of water, 1 teaspoon salt and 1 tablespoon of peanut oil for 5 to 7 minutes. Run cold water over cooked dumplings and drain. Serve immediately.

Serving Suggestion: I recommend Ginger Soy Sauce (page 38) as a dip with these dumplings.

Note: *Soi Gau* can be kept refrigerated for about 7 days or frozen for about 3 months. If you plan to freeze them for future use, undercook them by 2 minutes, drain, and dry them before freezing. To recook, defrost thoroughly, then steam them for 3 to 4 minutes. When freezing wrap them in plastic wrap, then in foil. They may also be heated in boiling water for 2 minutes.

Har Yuk Soi Gau

Shrimp Water Dumplings

The Chinese love shrimp, in all of its forms. In general, most dim sum use shrimp either alone or in some sort of combination, most often with pork. This dumpling, however, called Har Yuk, *or "shrimp meat," uses shrimp only, and it is quite different indeed from the traditional* Soi Gau.

$^3/_4$ pound shrimp, shelled, deveined, washed, dried, diced

3 fresh water chestnuts, peeled, cut into $^1/_8$-inch dice ($^1/_3$ cup)

$^1/_3$ cup scallions, white portions, finely sliced

1 teaspoon minced ginger

1 teaspoon light soy sauce

$^1/_2$ teaspoon salt

1$^1/_2$ teaspoons sugar

1 teaspoon sesame oil

1 teaspoon Shao-Hsing wine or sherry

1$^1/_2$ tablespoons oyster sauce

1$^1/_2$ tablespoons Scallion Oil (page 36)

1$^1/_2$ tablespoons cornstarch

1 egg white beaten

Pinch white pepper

1 Wheat Flour Dough recipe (page 64) or 24 commercial skins

To Boil Dumplings

2 quarts cold water

1 teaspoon salt

1 tablespoon peanut oil

Makes 24 dumplings

1. Make the filling: In a bowl combine the shrimp and all other ingredients (except egg white, skins, and boiling ingredients). Mix thoroughly until well blended. Remove to a shallow dish and refrigerate 4 hours, uncovered.

2. Make the dumplings: With kitchen shears or cookie cutter cut

skins to rounds of 2¼ inches in diameter. Place 1 tablespoon of filling in the center of the skin. With a butter knife brush egg around the outer edge of skin. Fold skin into half-moon shapes and press together along the curved edge tightly with thumb and forefinger to seal. Continue until all dumplings are made.

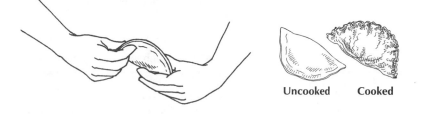

Uncooked   Cooked

3. Cook dumplings in 2 quarts of boiling water, 1 teaspoon salt, and 1 tablespoon peanut oil, for 5 to 7 minutes. Run cold water over cooked dumplings and drain. Serve immediately.

Serving Suggestion: These dumplings are complemented nicely with Vinegar Soy Sauce (page 38) as a dip.

Note: These dumplings may be kept refrigerated for about 2 days or frozen for about 3 months. If you plan to freeze them for future use, undercook by 2 minutes, drain, and dry before freezing. To recook, defrost thoroughly and steam for 3 to 4 minutes. When freezing, wrap dumplings in plastic wrap, then in foil. They may also be heated in boiling water for 2 minutes.

Red Oil Dumplings

Hung Yau Soi Gau

These are also known as Szechuan dumplings, because one of their ingredients is the red oil so favored by the chefs of Szechuan. The dumpling is shaped like a water dumpling, a dim sum of southern China, a good example of felicitous regional border crossing.

1/2	pound bok choy, washed, dried, stalks cut into 1/2-inch squares, the leaves into 1-inch squares
4	cups cold water
1/4	teaspoon baking soda (optional; see page 18)
1	teaspoon salt
1	slice ginger, 1/2 inch thick
1/2	pound lean ground beef

Filling Ingredients

1 1/2	teaspoons Red Oil (page 44)
1	teaspoon grated ginger
1 1/2	tablespoons oyster sauce
1	teaspoon sesame oil
1	teaspoon light soy sauce
1	teaspoon dark soy sauce
2	teaspoons Shao-Hsing wine or sherry
1 1/2	teaspoons sugar
1/4	teaspoon salt
2	tablespoons cornstarch
	Pinch of white pepper
3	tablespoons finely chopped fresh coriander
1	Wheat Flour Dough recipe (page 64) or 24 commercial skins

To Boil Dumplings

2	quarts cold water
1	teaspoon salt
1	tablespoon peanut oil

Makes 24 dumplings

1. Water blanch the bok choy: In a large pot place 4 cups of cold water, the baking soda, salt, and ginger. Bring to a boil over high heat. Add bok choy stalks. Stir and cook for 1 minute. Add leaves, stir, and cook for 1 minute more. Turn off heat. Run cold water into pot. Drain thoroughly, discard ginger. Reserve.

2. Make the filling: In a bowl place the ground beef and all other ingredients (except the skins and boiling ingredients). Mix thoroughly until well blended. Add bok choy and mix together well. Place in a shallow dish and refrigerate for 4 hours, uncovered.

3. Make the dumplings: With kitchen shears or a cookie cutter cut skins into rounds 3¼ inches in diameter. In center of each skin place 1 tablespoon of filling. Brush edges of skin with water. Fold skin into a half-moon shape and press together along the curved edge tightly with thumb and forefinger to seal. Continue until all dumplings are made.

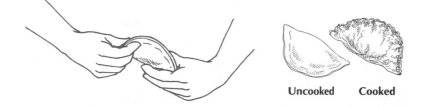

Uncooked   Cooked

4. Cook dumplings in 2 quarts of boiling water, 1 teaspoon salt, and 1 tablespoon peanut oil for 5 to 7 minutes. Run cold water over cooked dumplings and drain. Serve immediately.

Serving Suggestion: These dumplings are best served with drops of Red Oil (page 44).

Note: These dumplings may not be frozen.

Gai Yuk Soi Gau

Chicken *Soi Gau*

These are a classic of the Chinese teahouse and a treasured dumpling. Traditionally in China chicken was extremely expensive, and these dim sum were prized and not always available. Happily, we in the United States have no such limitations.

$^3/_4$ cup Tientsin bok choy stems, and 2 cups of
          leaves, both cut into $^1/_2$-inch pieces and
          packed tightly ($^1/_2$ pound)

4 cups cold water

$^1/_2$ teaspoon salt

$^1/_2$ pound chicken cutlet, coarsely ground

2 teaspoons sesame oil

2 scallions, ends discarded, finely sliced

$^1/_2$ teaspoon ginger juice (page 26) mixed with
          1 teaspoon Shao-Hsing wine or sherry

$1^1/_2$ tablespoons oyster sauce

1 teaspoon light soy sauce

$1^1/_4$ teaspoons sugar

$^1/_4$ teaspoon salt

$1^1/_2$ tablespoons cornstarch
          Pinch of white pepper

1 Wheat Flour Dough recipe (page 64) or
          24 commercial skins

To Boil Dumplings

2 quarts cold water

1 teaspoon salt

1 tablespoon peanut oil

Makes 24 dumplings

1. Water blanch the Tientsin bok choy: Place water and salt in large pot. Bring to a boil. Add Tientsin bok choy stems, stir, and cook for 30 seconds. Add leaves and allow to come to a boil, about 1 minute. Turn off heat. Run cold water into pot. Drain thoroughly all of the water. Reserve.

2. In a large bowl combine the chicken, the reserved Tientsin bok

choy, and all other ingredients (except the skins and the boiling ingredients) and mix thoroughly until well blended. Place in a shallow dish and refrigerate for 4 hours, uncovered.

3. Make the dumplings: With kitchen shears or cookie cutter cut skins into rounds 3¼ inches in diameter. Place 3 teaspoons of filling in the center of the skin, touch the edges with water. Fold skin into a half-moon shape and press together along curved edge tightly with thumb and forefinger to seal. Repeat until all dumplings are made. (As your proficiency grows increase filling amounts to 4 teaspoons).

Uncooked   Cooked

4. Cook the dumplings in 2 quarts of boiling water, 1 teaspoon salt, and 1 tablespoon of peanut oil for 5 to 6 minutes. Turn off heat, run cold water into pot over cooked dumplings, and drain. Serve immediately.

Serving Suggestion: These dumplings are best presented with a couple of drops of Hot Oil (page 37).

Note: These dumplings may not be frozen.

Cockscomb Dumplings

Gai Gun Gau

These Cantonese dumplings are sculpted to resemble the crest of the rooster. Usually they are filled with pork, shrimp, water chestnuts, and bamboo shoots. I re-created this version with veal a few years ago for a German wine maker who wanted a new dumpling to celebrate the Chinese Year of the Rooster.

¹/₂	pound lean ground veal (or ground chicken or turkey)
3	scallions, ends removed, finely sliced (1 cup)
¹/₄	cup jícama, cut into ¹/₈-inch dice
1	teaspoon grated ginger mixed with 2 teaspoons Shao-Hsing wine or sherry
¹/₂	teaspoon salt
1¹/₂	teaspoons sugar
³/₄	teaspoon light soy sauce
2	teaspoons sesame oil
1	tablespoon Garlic Oil (page 39)
1¹/₂	tablespoons oyster sauce
1	tablespoon Chicken Broth (page 33)
1¹/₂	tablespoons cornstarch
	Pinch of white pepper
1	Wheat Flour Dough recipe (page 64) or 22 commercial skins

To Boil Dumplings

2	quarts cold water
1	teaspoon salt
1	tablespoon peanut oil

Makes 22 dumplings

1. Make the filling: In a large bowl place the veal and all other ingredients (except the skins and the boiling ingredients). Mix thoroughly until well blended. Place in a shallow dish and refrigerate for 4 hours, uncovered.

2. Make the dumplings: With kitchen shears or a cookie cutter cut skins into rounds 3¹/₄ inches in diameter. Place 1 tablespoon

of filling in center of the skin. Use a butter knife to press filling down, and with the knife moisten the entire edge with water. Fold the skin into a half-moon and press edges together with thumb and forefinger to seal.

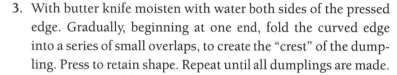

3. With butter knife moisten with water both sides of the pressed edge. Gradually, beginning at one end, fold the curved edge into a series of small overlaps, to create the "crest" of the dumpling. Press to retain shape. Repeat until all dumplings are made.
4. Bring the water, salt, and peanut oil to a boil and cook dumplings in the boiling water for 5 minutes. Run cold water over cooked dumplings, drain, and serve immediately.

Serving Suggestion: These dumplings go well with Ginger Soy Sauce (page 38) as a dip.

Note: These dumplings will keep for 2 or 3 days refrigerated. They may be frozen, wrapped in 2 layers of plastic wrap and then in foil. They will keep as long as 2 or 3 days. If you plan to freeze them for future use, undercook them by 2 minutes, drain, and dry before freezing. To recook, defrost thoroughly, then steam for 3 to 4 minutes. They may also be heated in boiling water for 2 minutes.

Chapter 4

Welcome Gifts from Shanghai

上海禮物

We have the chefs of Shanghai to thank for broadening the variety of the dim sum kitchen. Once cut into a network of European trading enclaves, Shanghai was quick to adopt, and adapt, aspects of Western cookery. It was the first place in China to produce the tiered wedding cake as an ornament of the Chinese kitchen. It was the chefs from Shanghai who baked Western breads, pastries, and sweets, later adapting many of these to the dim sum teahouse. Many exotic and ornamental dumplings also had their origins in Shanghai.

The following are the best of Shanghai, many recognized because they have been named for the city where they originated. All have become part of the dim sum dumpling repertoire and tradition, which continues to grow and develop, even today.

上海鍋貼

Wor Tip

Shanghai Potsticker Dumplings

These most famous of Shanghai dumplings are called Wor Tip, *two words that translate as "pot" and "stick." It is said that a cook of the emperor was making dumplings one day and forgot them on the stove. They burned, and the chef, fearing he might be beheaded if he admitted to carelessness, presented his emperor with a "new" dumpling. "Potsticker" is actually not a pretty name for something that tastes so good. They are known even in Beijing, where they are called* chiao-tzu, *which in Cantonese is pronounced "gau ji," or "little dumplings," a far more pleasant name.*

³/₄ **pound bok choy, separated into stalks and leaves, each cut into ¹/₂-inch pieces**
4 **cups water**
¹/₂ **teaspoon salt**
¹/₂ **teaspoon baking soda (optional; see Water Blanching, page 18)**
10 **ounces lean ground pork**
1 **scallion, finely sliced (¹/₃ cup)**
¹/₂ **teaspoon salt**
2 **teaspoons sugar**
1¹/₂ **teaspoons minced ginger**
1¹/₂ **teaspoons Shao-Hsing wine or sherry**
1 **teaspoon light soy sauce**
2 **teaspoons sesame oil**
1 **medium egg, beaten**
1 **tablespoon oyster sauce**
2 **tablespoons cornstarch**
Pinch of white pepper
1 **package Shanghai Dumpling Skins (see note)**
5 **tablespoons peanut oil**
1 **cup cold water**

Makes 34 dumplings

1. Water blanch the bok choy: In a pot over high heat bring 4 cups of water to a boil with salt and baking soda. Add bok choy

stalks, stir, and cook for 1 minute. Add leaves, stir, cook another minute. Turn off heat. Run cold water into pot over bok choy, drain. Squeeze in paper towel to dry.

2. Make the filling: In a bowl combine the pork, bok choy, and all other ingredients (except the skins, peanut oil, and water). Mix thoroughly to blend well. Refrigerate uncovered for 4 hours.

3. Make the dumplings: Spread about 1½ teaspoons of filling down the center of a round wrapper. Wet the edge of the wrapper with water. Fold into a half-moon shape, pleating as you seal the wrapper. Pinch the pleating to seal. Press one side of the dumpling against the fleshy part of your hand to flatten it slightly and create the classic potsticker shape. Repeat until all dumplings are made. As you work, the skins not in use should be kept covered with a damp cloth, so they will remain soft and pliable.

4. To fry each batch of dumplings, heat 3 tablespoons of the peanut oil in a large, cast iron skillet over high heat until a wisp of white smoke appears. Arrange 3 rows of dumplings in the skillet, 5 or 6 in a row; they may be touching lightly. Cook for 3 minutes. Pour ½ cup of cold water into skillet, reduce heat to moderate, and cook until all of the water has evaporated.

5. Reduce the heat to low and continue to cook, rotating the pan to distribute evenly, until the dumplings are golden brown on the bottom and somewhat translucent on top, 1 to 2 minutes longer. Remove dumplings from skillet and drain on paper towels. Repeat with second batch until all dumplings are made. Serve hot.

Serving Suggestion: These go quite nicely with Vinegar Soy Sauce (page 38) or with Vinegar Ginger Dip (page 45).

Note: I recommend two different dumpling skins to make potstickers. The first are labeled "Twin Dragon," are round, manufactured in Los Angeles, and can be found in the frozen food sections of Asian groceries. Another brand, also round, is labeled "Twin Marquis, Dumpling Wrappers, Shanghai Style." They are found in the refrigerated cases of groceries. They are not frozen. Both come in one-pound packs and are made without eggs, making them different from the usual won ton wrappers. The "Twin Dragon" skins, once defrosted, cannot be refrozen. The "Twin Marquis" can be refrozen. They will keep, wrapped in plastic wrap and foil, for two months. Defrost completely to room temperature before using.

Note: I prefer that these potstickers not be frozen because dumplings containing leafy vegetables often tend to lose their shape after defrosting. However, should you choose to freeze them, they should be frozen following step No. 3, after they have been formed, but not cooked. Before freezing dust the dumplings liberally with cornstarch, then double-wrap in plastic wrap and then in foil. They will keep, frozen, for two months. To cook allow to defrost and come to room temperature before proceeding with steps No. 4 and 5.

Gai Bin Gau

Shanghai Street Dumplings

These dumplings were created by the Shanghai refugees who fled their city in the 1950s after the revolution and came to Hong Kong. They would set up portable charcoal or coal stoves in the streets and make them for people to lunch on. These dumplings are rarely found these days, but I think a bit of culinary history is in order, particularly because they were so popular and tasty.

$^1/_2$ **pound bok choy, separated into stalks and leaves, each cut into $^1/_2$-inch pieces**

3 **cups cold water**

$^1/_2$ **teaspoon baking soda (optional; see page 18)**

$^1/_2$ **teaspoon salt**

$^1/_2$ **pound ground lean pork**

1 **tablespoon minced young ginger or $^1/_2$ tablespoon regular ginger**

1 **teaspoon sesame oil**

1 **teaspoon white vinegar**

$1^1/_2$ **teaspoons sugar**

$^1/_4$ **teaspoon salt**

1 **tablespoon oyster sauce**

Pinch white pepper

16 **won ton skin wrappers, square, $3^1/_4$–$3^1/_2$ inches to a side**

4 **tablespoons peanut oil**

$^2/_3$ **cup cold water**

Makes 16 dumplings

1. In a large pot, over high heat bring 3 cups of water to a boil with baking soda and salt. Add bok choy stems, stir, and cook for 1 minute. Add leaves, stir, and cook for another minute. Turn off heat. Run cold water into pot over bok choy. Drain, dry thoroughly with paper towels.

2. Make filling: Combine ground pork, bok choy, and all other
    ingredients (except wrappers, peanut oil, and cold water). Mix
    thoroughly to blend well. Refrigerate, uncovered, for 4 hours.

3. Make the dumplings: Place 1 tablespoon of filling in center of
    the skin. Use a butter knife to wet edges of skin. Pick up two
    opposite corners of skin, bring together and squeeze, to seal
    and create a triangle. Pick up other two opposite corners and
    squeeze them together with the first two. This will create a
    knob shape. Twist the dough at the point of closure. Turn dump-
    ling over and shape it into a round bundle, sealed side down.
    Repeat until all dumplings are formed. As you work, keep skins
    not in use under a damp cloth to retain their softness and pli-
    ability.

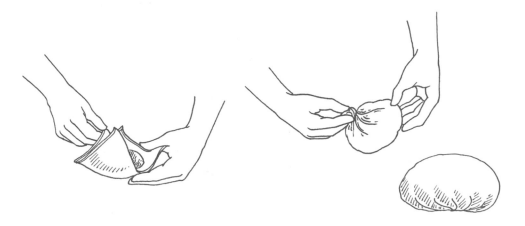

4. To fry each batch of dumplings, heat 2 tablespoons of peanut
    oil in a large, cast iron skillet over high heat until a wisp of
    white smoke appears. Place 8 dumplings at a time in skillet.
    Cook for 3 minutes. Pour ⅓ cup of cold water into skillet,
    reduce heat to moderate, and cook until all of the water has
    evaporated.

5. Reduce the heat to low and continue to cook, rotating the pan to distribute the heat evenly, until the dumplings are golden brown on the bottom and somewhat translucent on top, 1 to 2 minutes longer. Remove dumplings from skillet and drain on paper towels. Repeat with second batch, using remaining 2 tablespoons of peanut oil and ⅓ cup of water, until all dumplings are made. Serve hot.

Serving Suggestion: Serve these with Vinegar Soy Sauce (page 38) or with Vinegar Ginger Dip (page 45).

Note: I prefer that these dumplings not be frozen.

Soup Buns

Siu Loon Bau

The traditional method of making these buns was to cook fresh pig skin in water for 36 to 48 hours so that the skin dissolved in the resulting soup. When it cooled, it became a gelatin. But because this takes an enormous amount of time and the prospect of cooking pig skin for two days might not be all that pleasing to some, I use gelatin.

These buns, made here with a fresh chicken broth base, are possibly the most sought after dim sum of Shanghai, and justly so. Each bun, when steamed, contains a measure of liquid hot soup and the explosion of taste in one's mouth is exquisite. Very seldom do soup buns appear on dim sum menus because they take much time to prepare. But the results of these labors are most satisfying. Because many steps are involved, I recommend that you do many of them in advance, as I specify, and then combine them with a fresh dough.

2	cups Chicken Broth (page 33)
1	envelope unflavored gelatin
6	ounces lean ground pork
3	ounces shrimp, shelled, deveined, washed, dried, diced
1/2	teaspoon salt
1	teaspoon grated ginger
1 1/2	teaspoons sesame oil
1	teaspoon light soy sauce
1 1/4	teaspoons sugar
2	teaspoons Shao-Hsing wine or sherry
2	tablespoons beaten egg
1	tablespoon cornstarch
	Pinch of white pepper

Dough Ingredients

$2/3$ **cup flour (Pillsbury Best All-Purpose, bleached, enriched preferred)**

$1/4$ **teaspoon baking soda**

1 **egg**

$1/8$ **cup same flour as above mixed with $1/8$ cup boiling water**

Vegetable leaves

Makes 20 buns

1. Cook the chicken broth in a pot over medium heat, until reduced to 1 cup, about 20 minutes. Pour envelope of gelatin into a bowl and pour in boiling broth. Stir, mix well, and allow to cool to room temperature. Refrigerate and allow to set, about 3 to 4 hours. (This may be done the day before preparation.)

2. Make the filling: In a bowl combine the pork, shrimp, and all other ingredients (except the dough ingredients). Mix thoroughly to blend evenly. Cut the gelatin into a coarse dice, about $1/3$-inch pieces, and add to mixture. Mix again well to combine all ingredients. Place the bowl in the refrigerator overnight, covered. (This too is best done the night before.)

3. Make the dough: Mix the $2/3$ cup of flour and the baking soda with the egg and mix well. Make a well in the mixture and pour in the flour–boiling water mixture. Begin kneading the mass, dusting regularly with additional flour to prevent excessive stickiness. Knead into an elastic dough that is even in color and not streaked. When smooth, knead for 10 minutes, then set aside. Cover the dough with plastic wrap and allow it to rest, for 1 hour in summer, 2 hours in winter.

4. Make the dumplings: Cut the dough into 2 equal pieces. Roll each section into a sausage shape 10 inches long, and cut into 10 one-inch segments. Work on one piece at a time, keeping the remaining covered with plastic wrap. Using a small rolling pin, roll each small piece of dough into a thin 3-inch round (to avoid sticking, sprinkle cornstarch on the work surface). Place a round in your hand, put 1 tablespoon of filling in the center, and close the round.

Turn the piece and seal it by pleating it until it is round and closed, except for a tiny hole in the center. This hole is necessary to allow the steam to escape. Repeat until all buns are made. Place them in a steamer lined with vegetable leaves (that have been water blanched for 30 seconds). Steam for 12 minutes. Serve hot.

Serving Suggestion: Serve these with Vinegar Ginger Dip (page 45)

Note: Soup buns cannot be frozen, and they should not even be kept overnight in the refrigerator, because the skin will crack and the soup will run out. They should be served immediately and eaten at one meal.

Soup Dumplings

Gun Tong Gau

Though these are identical to the soup buns in terms of ingredients, they differ in shape, and they are easier to form. This soup dumpling shape is more likely to be found in the Cantonese dumpling house, but its owes its origins to Shanghai.

2 cups Chicken Broth (page 33)
1 envelope unflavored gelatin
6 ounces lean ground pork
3 ounces shrimp, shelled, deveined, washed, dried, diced
1/2 teaspoon salt
1 teaspoon grated ginger
1 1/2 teaspoons sesame oil
1 teaspoon light soy sauce
1 1/4 teaspoons sugar
2 teaspoons Shao-Hsing wine or sherry
2 tablespoons beaten egg
1 tablespoon cornstarch
Pinch of white pepper

Dough Ingredients

2/3 cup flour (Pillsbury Best All-Purpose, bleached, enriched preferred)
1/4 teaspoon baking soda
1 egg
1/8 cup same flour as above mixed with 1/8 cup boiling water
Vegetable leaves

Makes 20 dumplings

1. Cook the chicken broth in a pot over medium heat until reduced to 1 cup, about 20 minutes. Pour envelope of gelatin into a bowl and pour in boiling broth. Stir, mix well, and allow to cool to room temperature. Refrigerate and allow to set, about 3 to 4 hours. (This may be done the day before preparation.)

2. Make the filling: In a bowl combine the pork, shrimp, and all

other ingredients (except the dough ingredients). Mix thoroughly to blend well. Cut the gelatin into a coarse dice of about $1/3$-inch pieces, and add to mixture. Mix again well to combine all ingredients. Place the bowl in the refrigerator overnight, covered. (This too is best done the night before.)

3. Make the dough: Mix the $2/3$ cup of flour and baking soda with the egg and mix well. Make a well in the mixture and pour in the flour–boiling water mixture. Begin kneading the mass, dusting regularly with additional flour to prevent excessive stickiness. Knead into an elastic dough that is even in color and not streaked. When smooth, knead for 10 minutes, then set aside. Cover the dough with the plastic wrap and allow it to rest, for 1 hour in summer, 2 hours in winter.

4. Make the dumplings: Cut the dough into 2 equal pieces. Roll each into a sausage shape 10 inches long, and cut each of these into 10 one-inch segments. Work on one piece at a time, keeping the remaining covered with plastic wrap. Using a small rolling pin, roll each small piece of dough into a thin 3-inch round (to avoid sticking, sprinkle cornstarch on the work surface). Place a round in your hand; place $1\frac{1}{2}$ tablespoons of filling in center of round.

Fold in half and seal the entire curved edge, except for a $1/2$-inch hole in the center of the seam on top. Then place

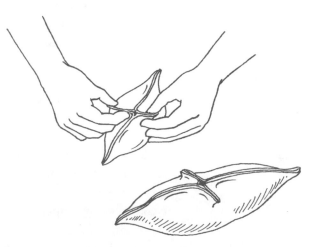

fingers on the opposite sides of the hole and, pulling gently, make another partial pleat, just sufficient to make the hole firm. The dumpling should be egg-shaped, flat on the bottom, with the hole secured by four pleats. (The reason for the hole is to allow steam to escape.)

5. Repeat until all dumplings are made. Place them in a steamer, hole sides up, the steamer lined with vegetable leaves (that have been water blanched for 30 seconds). Steam for 12 minutes. Serve hot.

Serving Suggestion: Serve these with Vinegar Ginger Dip (page 45).

Note: These dumplings cannot be frozen.

Seut Choi Gau

Snow Cabbage Dumplings

This unusual dumpling is highly prized in Shanghai, where it was created, and in Taiwan, where it migrated. Snow cabbage is called seut loi hung, *or "red in snow," although it is green. It is a leafy vegetable that is never eaten fresh, but is always cured in salt, then canned. The other main ingredient in this dumpling is Szechuan mustard pickle, the preserved root of mustard green. It was the master chefs of Shanghai who put these together so well.*

$\frac{1}{2}$ **pound lean ground pork**

$\frac{1}{4}$ **cup snow cabbage, washed, drained, cut into $\frac{1}{4}$-inch pieces**

1   **tablespoon Szechuan mustard pickle, minced**

$\frac{1}{4}$ **cup fresh water chestnuts, peeled, cut into $\frac{1}{8}$-inch dice (2 or 3)**

2   **scallions, both ends discarded, finely sliced**

$\frac{1}{4}$ **cup carrot, peeled, cut into $\frac{1}{8}$-inch dice**

$1\frac{1}{2}$ **teaspoons sesame oil**

1   **teaspoon light soy sauce**

1   **tablespoon oyster sauce**

$1\frac{1}{4}$ **teaspoons minced ginger**

3   **teaspoons Shao-Hsing wine or sherry**

1   **teaspoon minced garlic**

$1\frac{3}{4}$ **teaspoons sugar**

    Pinch of white pepper

4   **teaspoons cornstarch**

$\frac{1}{4}$ **teaspoon salt**

24   **won ton wrappers**

To Boil Dumplings

8   **cups cold water**

1   **teaspoon salt**

1   **tablespoon peanut oil**

Makes 24 dumplings

1. Make the filling: Place ground pork in bowl and add all other ingredients (except wrappers, cold water, 1 teaspoon salt, and peanut oil). Mix thoroughly to blend well. Refrigerate for 4 hours, uncovered.

2. Make the dumplings: With kitchen shears or a cookie cutter cut each skin into a round 3 inches in diameter. Place 1 tablespoon of filling in center of skin. With a butter knife spread water around outer edge of skin. Fold skin into a half-moon shape and press together tightly with thumb and forefinger to seal. Continue to make until all dumplings are made.

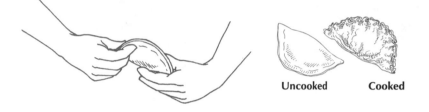

Uncooked   **Cooked**

3. Bring cold water, salt, and peanut oil to a boil and cook the dumplings for 5 to 6 minutes. Turn heat off. Run cold water into pot and drain. Serve immediately.

Serving Suggestion: I prefer Vinegar Soy Sauce (page 38) as a dip with these dumplings.

Note: Snow Cabbage Dumplings may be kept refrigerated for 3 days. They can be frozen for about 3 months. If you plan to freeze them for future use, undercook them by 2 minutes, drain, and dry. Wrap them in a double layer of plastic wrap, then in foil to freeze. To recook, defrost thoroughly, then steam for 3 to 4 minutes.

Chung Yau Bang

Scallion Pancakes

Scallion Pancakes are a very special dim sum of Shanghai. The Cantonese have nothing with which to compare it. When a Cantonese is asked about dim sum, his or her mind moves naturally to such dumplings as Har Gau *and* Siu Mai, *but to somebody from Shanghai, dim sum is lusty and savory Scallion Pancakes.*

1½ cups scallions, ends discarded, finely sliced

¾ teaspoon salt

1 teaspoon sugar

½ cup vegetable shortening

1½ cups Pillsbury Best All-Purpose Flour, bleached, enriched

4 ounces hot water (plus another ½ ounce in reserve, if needed)

1/2 cup peanut oil

Makes 10 pancakes

1. Make the filling: In a bowl make a paste of the scallions, salt, sugar, and vegetable shortening. Reserve in refrigerator, covered, for 4 hours.

2. Prepare the dough: Mound flour on work surface. Make a well and pour in the hot water with one hand, using fingers of the other hand to mix. When all the water has been poured, knead flour and water into dough. (If dough is too dry, add the reserved water.)

   Using a scraper pick up the dough and continue to knead for 5 to 7 minutes, until the dough is smooth and elastic. Cover dough with a damp cloth and allow it to rest for at least 30 minutes.

3. Prepare the pancakes: Divide the dough into 2 equal pieces. To prevent sticking as you roll the dough, flour the work surface and rolling pin frequently. Roll each piece into a 12½-inch-long sausage shape. Cut each into 5 equal 2½-inch segments. With a rolling pin roll each segment out to a piece measuring 10 by 4 inches with rounded edges.

Spread 1½ tablespoons of filling along center of dough lengthwise. Fold both sides so that they meet over the filling. Then flatten gently to seal. Fold in half lengthwise again and press again. Pick up the dough by the ends and gently stretch it, hitting it gently on the work surface at the same time.

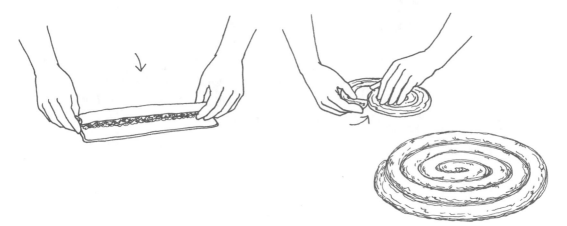

Placing the folded edge outward, bring the left end to the middle, creating a circle. Bring the right end around as far as possible to the left. Slip end between folds of dough and press gently. Press gently again so that the roll becomes a solid pancake. Repeat process until all pancakes are made.

4. Using ¼ cup of the peanut oil, fry the pancakes in the oil in a large cast iron skillet, 5 at a time, until golden brown on both sides. Repeat with second batch. Add remaining peanut oil. Remove the pancakes, drain, and serve immediately.

Serving Suggestion: The pungency of the scallions needs no accompaniment.

Note: Both the dough and the filling can be made a day ahead and refrigerated. The filling can be frozen and stored for 1 to 2 months. Cooked Scallion Pancakes can be frozen for 1 to 2 months. Double-wrap them in plastic wrap, then in foil, for freezing. To reheat, allow to defrost to room temperature, then pan-fry or reheat in a 350°F oven until heated through.

Fred's Special Scallion Pancakes

Fu Lit Yau Bang

This large scallion pancake is served most often in restaurants, generally because it requires a bit less effort to make than the smaller Scallion Pancakes. Instead of individual pancakes, this recipe produces 2 pie-sized pancakes that are cut into wedges for serving. The dough preparation is identical to that for the small Scallion Pancakes, and so is the filling, except for the addition of diced Chinese sausages, which is my husband's suggestion.

1½ **cups scallions, ends discarded, finely sliced**
¾ **teaspoon salt**
1 **teaspoon sugar**
½ **cup vegetable shortening**
1½ **cups Pillsbury Best All-Purpose Flour, bleached, enriched**
4 **ounces hot water (plus another ½ ounce in reserve, if needed)**
½ **cup Chinese sausage, cut into ⅛-inch dice**
1/4 **cup peanut oil**

Makes 2 pancakes

1. Make the filling: In a bowl make a paste of the scallions, salt, sugar, and vegetable shortening. Reserve in refrigerator, covered, for 4 hours.

2. Prepare the dough: Mound flour on work surface. Make a well and pour in the hot water with one hand, using fingers of the other hand to mix. When all the water has been poured, knead flour and water into dough. (If dough is too dry, add the reserved water.) Using a scraper, pick up the dough and continue to knead for 5 to 7 minutes, until the dough is smooth and elastic. Cover dough with a damp cloth and allow it to rest for at least 30 minutes.

3. Prepare the pancakes: Divide the dough into 2 equal pieces. Work with one piece; keep the other covered with a damp cloth. With your hands roll the piece of dough into a ball, then press

down with your palm. Make certain the work surface is dusted with flour to prevent sticking. With a rolling pin, roll out the dough to a round 9 inches in diameter.

Spread 3½ tablespoons of filling evenly over the dough, leaving a ½-inch border. Then sprinkle half of the diced Chinese sausage on top and spread evenly. Begin at one side and roll the pancake into a sausage shape. Then roll the sausage, jelly-roll fashion, into a round. Close the end by pressing down. Repeat process with remaining dough, filling, and sausage.

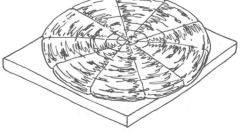

4. Using 2 tablespoons of peanut oil, fry one pancake in a cast iron skillet over medium heat, 3 minutes on each side until golden brown. Remove from skillet, drain on a paper towel. Cut into wedges and serve immediately.

Serving Suggestion: No accompaniment needed.

Note: These special scallion pancakes can be frozen for 1 to 2 months. To reheat, allow to defrost to room temperature, then pan-fry or reheat in a 350°F oven until warmed through.

SHANGHAI PASTRIES

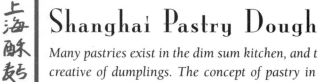

Shanghai Pastry Dough

Seung Hoi So Bang

Many pastries exist in the dim sum kitchen, and they are the most creative of dumplings. The concept of pastry in China is essentially from Shanghai, and it is the Shanghai chefs who developed many of the most well-known pastry dumplings, which were enthusiastically adopted by the master Cantonese dim sum chefs. Here is a basic, and quite simple, Shanghai pastry dough. It consists of two dough mixtures that are combined to give the pastry its flakiness.

Traditionally this dough was based on lard, as were so many fine breads in the past. However, I realize that there is resistance these days to lard, so I use peanut oil instead. You may notice that this dough might display a slight oily sheen, but this should not disturb you.

Dough Mixture 1
- ¹/₂ **cup Pillsbury Best Bread Flour, enriched, bromide**
- ¹/₂ **cup Pillsbury Best All-Purpose Flour, bleached, enriched**
- ¹/₂ **teaspoon salt (optional)**
- 1 **tablespoon peanut oil**
- ¹/₃ **cup hot water**

1. Place flour on work surface. Mix in salt. Make a well in the center. Add peanut oil and hot water slowly, and mix with the fingers. Working with a dough scraper, pick up dough and knead for 4 minutes, until it becomes cohesive and has elasticity. It should be very soft. Cover with a damp cloth. Set aside. Prepare dough mixture 2.

Dough Mixture 2   ¹/₂ **cup Pillsbury Best Bread Flour, enriched, bromide**

¹/₂ **cup Pillsbury Best All-Purpose Flour, bleached, enriched**

¹/₄ **teaspoon salt (optional)**

6 **tablespoons peanut oil**

1. Place flour on work surface. Mix in salt. Make a well in the center. Add peanut oil and work together with the fingers. Using a dough scraper, gather and knead dough, as described above. When smooth and soft, cover with a damp cloth and set aside.

2. Prepare pastry dough: Press mixture 1 with your hand into and 8-inch round. Place mixture 2 into the center. Gather up the edges to seal. Dust work surface lightly with flour and roll out dough to a rectangle, about 16 by 10 inches. Fold dough into thirds, overlapping.

   Roll to flatten and overlap again. Repeat twice more. The third rolling of the pastry dough should be to a rectangle 20 inches by 10 inches. With your hands roll dough along its width to arrive at a 20-inch-long sausage shape. Cover with plastic wrap to retain softness and pliability.

   The dough is now ready for use.

Note: This pastry dough should be made fresh each time it is to be used.

咖喱鸡酥餅

Gah Li Gai
So Bang

Curried Chicken Pastry

While experimenting with Shanghai Pastry Dough and with various fillings I hit upon this recipe. This traditional crescent-shaped pastry dumpling exists both in Shanghai and in Canton. Customarily it is filled with curried beef. I took the concept, made a chicken curry, and put this inside the dumpling. I am quite happy with the result, which combines tradition and newness.

$^1/_2$ **pound skinless, boneless chicken breast, cut into $^1/_4$-inch dice**

Marinade for Chicken

1 **teaspoon sesame oil**

1 **tablespoon oyster sauce**

$^3/_4$ **teaspoon salt**

1$^1/_2$ **teaspoons sugar**

1 **tablespoon cornstarch**

$^3/_4$ **teaspoon light soy sauce**
Pinch of white pepper

To Continue Recipe

$^1/_2$ **cup fresh water chestnuts, peeled, cut into $^1/_8$-inch dice**

$^1/_3$ **cup celery, cut into $^1/_8$-inch dice**

1 **tablespoon finely chopped fresh coriander**

$^3/_4$ **cup scallions, finely sliced**

2 **tablespoons curry powder (Madras brand preferred), mixed with 2 tablespoons cold water**

2 **tablespoons peanut oil**

2 **cloves garlic, minced**

1 **tablespoon Shao-Hsing wine or sherry**

1 **to 2 tablespoons Chicken Broth (page 33), if needed**

5 **cups peanut oil, for deep-frying**

1 **Shanghai Pastry Dough recipe (page 104)**

Makes 20 pastries

1. Prepare filling: Combine the marinade ingredients in a large bowl and marinate the chicken for 1 hour. Reserve. In a bowl combine water chestnuts, celery, coriander, and scallions. Reserve. Mix curry powder and water. Reserve.

2. Heat wok over high heat. Add 2 tablespoons peanut oil. Coat wok with spatula. When a wisp of white smoke appears add garlic, stir. When garlic turns light brown, add curry and water mixture. Raise heat and stir-fry for 1 to $1\frac{1}{2}$ minutes or until the curry releases its aroma. Add chicken and its marinade. Stir, then spread to a thin layer and cook for 30 seconds. Turn over and gently mix with the curry. Add the wine around the edge of the wok. Mix. Add vegetables and stir all together. If the mixture is too thick and dry, add the chicken broth. Stir.

3. Remove from wok, place in a shallow dish, and allow to come to room temperature. Refrigerate, uncovered, for 4 hours, or overnight, covered.

4. Make the pastries: Using Shanghai Pastry Dough recipe (page 104), cut the sausage shape into 20 equal pieces. Place one piece on work surface. Press down with your palm. Then with a small rolling pin (I find a 10-inch length of broomstick ideal) roll into a round $3\frac{1}{2}$ inches in diameter.

5. Place 1 tablespoon of curried chicken filling in the center of the round. Fold into a half-moon shape. Squeeze curved edge to seal; edge should be $\frac{1}{3}$-inch border. With side of your thumb press down on border to make a regular, decorative scalloped

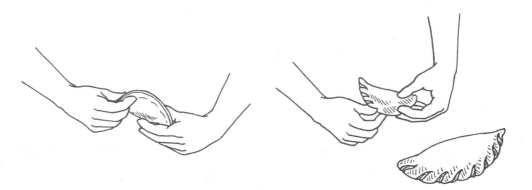

edge. Make one pastry at a time. Keep dough pieces as well as completed pastries covered with plastic wrap to keep moist. (Begin with 1 tablespoon of filling per pastry. As you become proficient increase to 1½ tablespoons.) When all pastries are made, prepare the wok.

6. In a wok heat the 5 cups of peanut oil to 325°F to 350°F. Place the pastries, in three batches, in a Chinese strainer and lower them into the hot oil. Deep-fry until golden brown, about 5 minutes, turning them frequently to ensure uniform color. Remove from heat and serve immediately.

Serving Suggestion: I prefer to eat these without any sauce or dip.

Note: I do not recommend freezing these pastries. They will keep, in a very cold refrigerator, up to 7 days.

Shanghai Shrimp Pastry

Seung Hoi Sin
Har So Bang

In general, shrimp are either minced, diced, or made into a paste for dim sum. Occasionally they are used whole; on occasion I have had Har Gau made with a whole shrimp rather than a minced filling. This truly modern dumpling—with whole shrimp, sun-dried tomatoes, and my own Garlic Oil, ingredients not normally found in the teahouse—has become a favorite of my family.

20 extra-large shrimp (²/₃ pound)

Marinade for Shrimp
2¹/₂ tablespoons Garlic Oil (page 39)
¹/₄ teaspoon salt
¹/₈ teaspoon white pepper
20 sun-dried tomatoes, washed if fresh, soaked
    in warm water for 1 minute if too dry to
    soften, each cut into 4 pieces

To Continue Recipe
1 beaten egg
1 Shanghai Pastry Dough recipe (page 104)
5 cups peanut oil, for deep-frying

Makes 20 pastries

1. Combine the marinade ingredients in a large bowl. Prepare shrimp: Peel, leaving intact the last section of shell at the tail and on the tail. Devein, wash, and dry thoroughly with paper towels. Place in dish with marinade and allow to stand for 15 minutes.

2. Prepare the pastries: Using Shanghai Pastry Dough recipe, cut the sausage shape into 10 equal pieces, each 2 inches long. Then cut each of these in half lengthwise, to create 20 pieces.

3. Roll each piece to 2³/₄ inches by 5 inches. Brush the entire rolled piece with beaten egg. Place shrimp at narrow end of rectangle. Place 2 pieces of sun-dried tomato on each side of shrimp. Roll tightly, making sure the tail of the shrimp protrudes from the roll. When rolled, press to seal and seal roll around the tail. Repeat until all pastries are made.

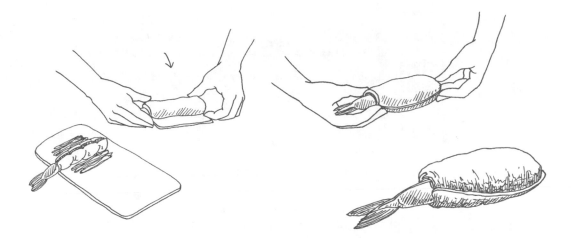

4. In a wok heat peanut oil to 325°F to 350°F. Place the pastries, in three batches, in a Chinese strainer and lower into hot oil. Deep-fry until golden brown, about 5 minutes, turning them frequently to ensure uniform color. Remove from heat and serve immediately.

Serving Suggestion: These shrimp pastries go very well with Sweet and Sour sauce (page 43) or with Curry Sauce (page 42).

Note: These pastries should not be frozen. They will keep, in a very cold refrigerator, for no more than 2 days.

Choi Yeun
So Bang

Garden Pastry

This vegetarian pastry is an example of jai, *which to the Chinese, Buddhists in particular, means foods without meat. Vegetable-filled pastries are common, in many combinations, in the dim sum kitchen. This pastry is customarily filled with turnips; I make it with my own collection of flavors and textures, wrapped in the Shanghai tradition.*

1½ teaspoons Garlic Oil (page 39)
⅛ teaspoon salt
2 scallions, both ends discarded, the white portion lightly smashed, cut into ¼-inch pieces (½ cup)
½ cup Chinese black mushrooms (7–8) steamed (page 166), then finely shredded
⅔ cup sweet red pepper (¾ of a medium pepper), finely shredded
½ cup fresh water chestnuts (4), peeled, shredded
⅓ cup ginger pickle (pages 26–27), finely shredded
1 tablespoon oyster sauce
2½ teaspoons tapioca flour mixed with 1 tablespoon cold water
1 Shanghai Pastry Dough recipe (page 104)
1 beaten egg
¼ cup white sesame seeds
5 cups peanut oil, to deep-fry pastries

Makes 20 pastries

1. Prepare the filling: Heat wok over high heat for 30 seconds. Add Garlic Oil and salt and coat wok with spatula. When a wisp of white smoke appears, add scallions. Stir and cook for 45 seconds. Add all other vegetables. Mix and cook for 1 minute. Add oyster sauce. Mix well, cooking for another minute. Stir

tapioca flour mixture, make a well in center of mixture, pour in. Mix thoroughly and cook for 30 seconds. Turn off heat. Transfer to a shallow dish and refrigerate, uncovered, for 4 hours or overnight.

2. Make the pastries: Using Shanghai Pastry Dough recipe, cut the sausage shape into 10 equal pieces, each 2 inches long. Then cut each of these in half lengthwise, to create 20 pieces.

3. Roll each piece into a square 4 by 4 inches. Place 1 tablespoon of filling in center. Pick up all sides and crimp closed. Twist dough to seal, then break off excess dough. Dip sealed side into beaten egg, then press into sesame seeds. Repeat until all pastries are made.

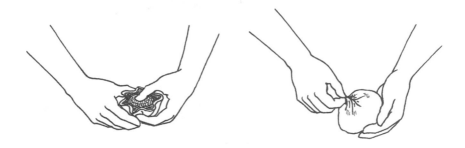

4. In a wok heat peanut oil to 325°F to 350°F. Place the pastries, in three batches, in a Chinese strainer and lower them into the hot oil. Deep-fry until golden brown, about 5 minutes, turning them frequently to ensure uniform color. Remove from heat and serve immediately.

Serving Suggestion: I recommend a few drops of Hot Oil (page 37) on these pastries.

Note: I do not recommend freezing these pastries. They will keep, about 3 days, in a very cold refrigerator.

Dau Sah So
Bang

Red Bean Pastry

This is a favorite dim sum from Shanghai that has become popular in Cantonese teahouses. In Shanghai it is a dim sum pastry dumpling; in Canton it is enjoyed as a light snack, with tea, or even as the final course in a banquet. The filling of sweetened cooked red bean paste is easily found in cans in Asian markets. I do not recommend you make the filling yourself, because it requires an enormous amount of time and much work, and the canned pastes are very good indeed; so good that dim sum chefs use these prepared pastes themselves.

1　**Shanghai Pastry Dough recipe (page 104)**
1　**can red bean paste**
1　**egg, beaten**
¹/₄　**cup black sesame seeds**
5　**cups peanut oil, for deep frying**

Makes 20 pastries

1. Make the pastries: Using the Shanghai Pastry Dough recipe, cut the sausage shape into 20 equal pieces, each 1 inch.
2. Roll each piece with a small rolling pin to a round 3¹/₂ inches in diameter. In the center of the round place 2 teaspoons of the red bean paste. Gather up the sides of the dough and with your fingers turn and crimp it until it becomes egg-shaped. Brush egg on the sealed side and press into black sesame seeds to coat that side. Repeat until all pastries are made.

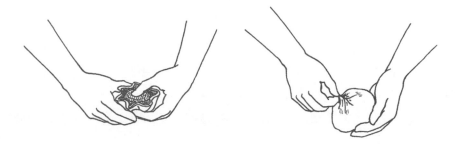

3. In a wok heat peanut oil to 325°F to 350°F. Place the pastries, in three batches, in a Chinese strainer and lower them into the hot oil. Deep-fry until golden brown, about 5 minutes, turning them frequently to ensure uniform color. Remove from heat and serve immediately.

Serving Suggestion: No accompaniment is needed for these pastries.

Note: These red bean pastries should not be frozen. They will keep, up to 3 days, in a very cold refrigerator.

Chapter 5

Buns: Steamed and Baked

Most breads in China are in the form of buns rather than loaves, though in Beijing small loaves are fashioned as well. And most of these buns are steamed, which is the way Chinese have traditionally prepared breads. Again, there was a variation in imperial Beijing, where occasionally steamed breads were also fried to create a thin, crisp crust.

In the north, in the wheat culture of Beijing and its surroundings, wheat rather than rice was the staple (although it was considered "grain food" or somewhat of a substitute for rice). It was milled into flour and then formed into noodles, cakes, and buns. Seldom were wheat doughs baked, though it is known that baking of a sort existed in China as early as the T'ang dynasty in the seventh century, and seven hundred years later in the court of the Mings where steamed and baked breads were served. These baked breads were quite like the *nan* of India, small breads baked usually on the sides of clay ovens.

Throughout most of China, however, steamed buns were the norm, and in both the north and south they were often enhanced with fillings. But it remained for the southern Chinese, in Canton, to make filled buns into an art and to create what is arguably the most famous filled bun ever, the steamed *Char Siu Bau*, a bun filled with seasoned roasted pork. The name of the bun was derived from its filling. *Char siu* translates literally as "fork-roasted pork," for the pork was roasted hung from a forklike projection in an oven; thus *Char Siu Bau* or "fork-roasted pork buns."

In Shanghai baking became an art, the result of the Western culinary influences that grew in importance as Western commercial enclaves spread. Bread loaves, cakes, pies, and even candies became common in Shanghai, and baking techniques spread through China. In Canton baking was adopted enthusiastically by the dim sum teahouses, where often baked buns replaced those that usually had been steamed. Again, it was the teahouse and its imaginative chefs who are responsible for the wide range of filled buns and dumplings that exist today.

Steamed Bun Dough

Jing Bau
Min Teun

This dough, with a bleached flour base, is ideal for several steamed varieties of dim sum buns, particularly Jing Char Siu Bau, *those roast pork–filled buns that become flowerlike as they steam. Once this dough has cooked through, it becomes soft and spongelike and complements its various fillings such as roast pork,* lop cheung *(Chinese pork sausages), and lotus seed paste.*

1¹/₈ cups flour (Gold Medal All-Purpose,
     enriched, bleached preferred; see note)
1³/₄ teaspoons baking powder
 ¹/₄ cup sugar
  3 tablespoons milk
  2 tablespoons water
1¹/₂ tablespoons peanut oil

1. Mix flour, baking powder, and sugar together on work surface. Make a well in the center and add milk. With fingers combine with flour mixture. After milk has been absorbed, add water and with fingers continue to work the dough. Add peanut oil and, again, continue to work the dough.

2. Using a dough scraper, gather the dough with one hand and begin kneading with the other. Knead for 10 minutes. If the dough is dry, sprinkle with water and continue to knead, until the dough becomes elastic. If the dough is wet, sprinkle a bit of flour on the work surface and on your hands and continue working.

3. When dough is elastic, cover with a damp cloth and allow to rest at least one hour. The dough is ready for use.

Note: Gold Medal All-Purpose Enriched and Bleached Flour is the best American flour for this dough. Bleached flour must be used to ensure the snowy white color.

Note: This dough must be used within 3 hours of the time it has been made. It cannot be frozen.

Jing Char
Siu Bau

Steamed Pork Buns

This is the dim sum bun I remember eating the first time my brother took me to a teahouse. Among the Cantonese, if you know you are going to a teahouse, then you know you must have Jing Char Siu Bau.

Sauce Ingredients		
	2	teaspoons oyster sauce
	³/₄	teaspoon dark soy sauce
	2	teaspoons ketchup
	1¹/₂	teaspoons sugar
		Pinch of white pepper
	3	tablespoons Chicken Broth (page 33)
	¹/₂	teaspoon sesame oil

To Continue Recipe		
	2	teaspoons peanut oil
	¹/₃	cup onions, cut into ¹/₄-inch dice
	¹/₂	cup Roast Pork (page 120)
	1	teaspoon Shao-Hsing wine or sherry
	1	Steamed Bun Dough recipe (page 117)

Makes 5 buns

1. Combine sauce ingredients above. Reserve. Prepare filling: Heat wok over high heat for 30 seconds. Add peanut oil and coat wok with spatula. When a wisp of white smoke appears, add onions, lower heat to low, and cook, turning occasionally, until onions turn light brown, 3 to 4 minutes. Add roast pork, raise heat, and stir-fry to combine the pork with the onions, about 1 minute. Add wine and mix well.

2. Lower heat, stir sauce mixture, and add to pork and onions. Stir until well mixed and sauce thickens and bubbles. Turn heat off. Remove mixture from wok and transfer to a shallow dish. Allow to cool to room temperature, then refrigerate for 4 hours, uncovered, or overnight, covered.

3. Prepare buns: Cut 8 squares of parchment paper (or waxed paper) into pieces 2¹/₂ inches by 2¹/₂ inches. Set aside.

4. Using dough in Steamed Bun Dough recipe roll dough into a cylindrical piece 8 inches long. Cut into 8 one-inch pieces. Roll each piece into a ball. Work with one piece at a time, covering pieces not being used with a damp cloth.

5. Press ball of dough down lightly; then, working with fingers of both hands, press dough into a domelike shape. Place 1 tablespoon of filling in center of well that has been created. Gather the dough, close, and pleat it with fingers until filling is completely enclosed. (As your proficiency grows increase filling to 2 tablespoons.) Twist, break off excess dough. The closure should be smooth.

6. Place buns on paper squares, closed, pleated side up, and place in a steamer at least 2 inches apart, to allow for expansion. Steam for 15 to 20 minutes. Serve immediately.

Serving Suggestion: No sauce or dip is recommended as an accompaniment.

Note: These buns may be frozen after cooking. They will keep 2 to 3 months. To reheat, defrost thoroughly and allow to come to room temperature. Then steam for 3 minutes, or until hot.

Roast Pork

Char Siu

This filling, for both steamed and baked pork buns, is also called "barbecued pork" by the Chinese. As a filling, it is particularly pungent and tasty indeed. However, it is equally satisfying by itself—hot, cold, or spiced up and stir-fried with vegetables. I call it my "all-purpose pork."

2¼ **pounds lean pork butt**
1½ **tablespoons dark soy sauce**
1½ **tablespoons light soy sauce**
1½ **tablespoons honey**
¼ **teaspoon salt**
1½ **tablespoons oyster sauce**
2 **tablespoons blended whiskey**
3½ **tablespoons hoisin sauce**
⅛ **teaspoon white pepper**
½ **teaspoon five-spice powder**

Makes about 3 cups

1. Cut pork into strips 1 inch thick and 7 inches long. Using a small knife, pierce the meat repeatedly at ½-inch intervals to help tenderize it.
2. Line a roasting pan with foil. Place the strips of meat in a single layer at the bottom of the roasting pan. Pour all the remaining ingredients, which have been mixed in a bowl, over the meat, and allow to marinate for 4 hours or overnight.
3. Preheat the oven to broil. Place the roasting pan in the oven

and roast for 30 to 50 minutes. To test the meat, remove one strip of pork after 30 minutes and slice it to see if it is cooked through. During the cooking period, meat should be basted 5 or 6 times and turned 4 times. If the sauce dries add water to the pan.

4. When the meat is cooked, allow it to cool, then refrigerate it until ready for use.

Note: Char Siu can be made ahead. It can be refrigerated 4 or 5 days, and it can be frozen for 1 month. Allow it to defrost before using.

Sahng Yuk Bau

Steamed Curried Pork Buns

These buns were created by one of the great master chefs of Canton, Chun Wing, in the 1930s. He traveled throughout China and wrote cookbooks about all of China's cuisines. He came later to Hong Kong and was a popular teacher for decades. He is credited with making wheat-based buns and dough more accepted in southern China. I have recreated this steamed bun from his repertoire.

	1/4 **pound pork fillet**
Pork Marinade	3/4 **teaspoon sesame oil**
	1/2 **teaspoon light soy sauce**
	1/4 **teaspoon double dark soy sauce**
	3/4 **teaspoon sugar**
	1/4 **teaspoon salt**
	1 **teaspoon oyster sauce**
	1 **teaspoon Shao-Hsing wine or sherry**
	1 **teaspoon cornstarch**
	Pinch of white pepper
Curry Paste	4 **teaspoons curry powder (Madras brand preferred) combined with**
	2 **tablespoons Chicken Broth (page 33)**
Sauce Ingredients	2 **teaspoons oyster sauce**
	2 **teaspoons cornstarch**
	1/4 **cup Chicken Broth (page 33)**
To Continue Recipe	2 1/2 **tablespoons peanut oil**
	1/2 **cup onions, cut into 1/4-inch dice**
	1/4 **cup sweet red peppers, cut into 1/4-inch dice**
	1 **teaspoon minced ginger**
	2 **tablespoons chopped fresh coriander**
	1 **teaspoon minced garlic**
	1 **Steamed Bun Dough recipe (page 117)**

Makes 8 buns

1. Prepare filling: Cut pork fillets into pieces $1/2$ inch square, thinly sliced. Combine the marinade ingredients, marinate the pork 30 minutes, and reserve. Combine the curry paste ingredients and reserve. Combine the sauce ingredients and reserve.

2. Heat wok over high heat for 30 seconds. Add 1 tablespoon of peanut oil and coat wok with spatula. When a wisp of white smoke appears add the diced onions, lower heat to medium, and stir and cook for 2 minutes until onions become translucent. Turn heat back to high, add the peppers, and stir-fry for 1 minute. Turn off heat. Remove onion and pepper mixture. Reserve. Wash and dry wok and spatula.

3. Heat wok over high heat for 30 seconds. Add remaining peanut oil and coat wok with spatula. When a wisp of white smoke appears add minced ginger. Stir. Add coriander and garlic and stir together. When garlic turns light brown add the curry paste and mix well. Cook for 1 minute until the curry aroma is released. Add pork and marinade. Spread in a thin layer and cook for 1 minute. Turn pork over and mix well. Add reserved onion and pepper mixture and stir together for 1 minute. Stir the sauce, make a well in the center of the mixture, and add sauce. Mix all together, cooking for 2 minutes, or until the sauce thickens. Turn off heat. Transfer to a shallow dish and allow to cool to room temperature. Refrigerate for 4 hours, uncovered, or overnight, covered.

4. Prepare buns: Follow procedures precisely, as in recipe for Steamed Pork Buns (page 118).

Serving Suggestion: No sauce or dip accompaniment is recommended for these buns. The curry taste is sufficient.

Note: These buns may be frozen after cooking. They will keep 2 to 3 months. To reheat, defrost thoroughly and allow to come to room temperature. Steam for 3 minutes, or until hot.

Lop Cheung
Guen

Steamed Sausage Buns

These steamed sausage buns are a winter treat in the dim sum teahouse, since the cured pork sausages with which they are made are manufactured only in the cooler months. Because we had to wait for them, they became doubly a treat for us as youngsters. These days there is no wait—lop cheung is always available.

> 4 cured Chinese pork sausages (*lop cheung*)
> 1½ tablespoons oyster sauce
> 1½ tablespoons dark soy sauce
> ½ tablespoon sesame oil
> 1 Steamed Bun Dough recipe (page 117)

Makes 8 buns

1. Cut sausages in half, lengthwise and diagonally. In a shallow dish, combine the oyster sauce, soy sauce, and sesame oil. Add the sausage and marinate for 30 minutes.
2. Cut 8 pieces of parchment paper (or waxed paper) into rectangles, 3½ by 2 inches. Set aside.
3. Using Steamed Bun Dough recipe, roll dough into a cylindrical piece 8 inches long. Cut into 8 one-inch pieces. Work with one piece at a time, covering the remaining pieces with a damp cloth. Roll pieces into sausage shapes 12 inches in length.

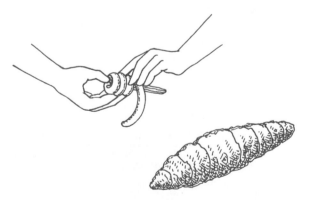

4. Hold the sausage piece by its thinly cut end together with one end of the 12-inch length of dough. Press, then wrap the dough around the sausage in a spiral until dough is rolled around the sausage piece. Place the rolls on the pieces of paper and place in a steamer 1 inch apart to allow for expansion. Steam for 15 to 20 minutes. Serve immediately.

Serving Suggestion: No sauce or dip is recommended as an accompaniment.

Note: These sausage rolls may be frozen after cooking. They will keep 2 to 3 months. To reheat, defrost thoroughly and allow to come to room temperature. Then steam for 3 minutes, or until hot.

Steamed Chicken

Buns Gai Bau

It was natural that the Chinese love for pork in their buns and dumplings would be followed by the use of chicken to enhance steamed buns. More elegant in the teahouse and more delicate than seasoned pork, Chicken was a happy combination with lighter teas. Occasionally this bun was made into what today would be considered a round loaf, filled with chicken and served to several people.

Marinade for Chicken

- 1/4 teaspoon grated ginger mixed with 1/2 teaspoon Shao-Hsing wine or sherry
- 1 teaspoon light soy sauce
- 1/2 teaspoon sesame oil
- 1/2 teaspoon sugar
- 1 1/2 teaspoons oyster sauce
- Pinch of white pepper
- 3/4 teaspoon cornstarch
- 1/4 pound skinless, boneless chicken breast, cut into 1/3-inch cubes

Sauce Ingredients

- 1 tablespoon oyster sauce
- 1/4 teaspoon light soy sauce
- 1/4 teaspoon dark soy sauce
- 1/2 teaspoon sesame oil
- 1/2 teaspoon sugar
- 1/8 teaspoon salt
- 2 teaspoons cornstarch
- Pinch of white pepper
- 3 tablespoons Chicken Broth (page 33)

To Continue Recipe

- 1 tablespoon peanut oil
- 1/4 cup Chinese black mushrooms, soaked in warm water for 30 minutes, cut into 1/4-inch pieces
- 1 tablespoon bamboo shoots, cut into 1/4-inch pieces

1¹/₂ teaspoons Shao-Hsing wine or sherry
1 large scallion, white portion, minced
  (¹/₈ cup)
1 Steamed Bun Dough recipe (page 117)

Makes 8 buns

1. Prepare filling: Combine the marinade ingredients and marinate chicken for 30 minutes. Reserve. Combine the sauce ingredients and reserve.

2. Heat wok over high heat for 30 seconds. Add 1 tablespoon of peanut oil and coat wok with spatula. When a wisp of white smoke appears add chicken and the marinade. Spread in a thin layer, cook for 30 seconds. Turn over and mix. Add mushrooms, bamboo shoots, stir, and cook for 1 minute. Add wine. Mix well. Add scallions and cook all together for 30 seconds. Make a well in the center of the mixture, stir sauce, and pour in. Mix thoroughly until sauce thickens and bubbles. Turn off heat. Transfer to a shallow dish and allow to come to room temperature. Refrigerate for 4 hours, uncovered, or overnight, covered.

3. Prepare buns: Follow procedures precisely as in recipe for Steamed Pork Buns (page 118).

Serving Suggestion: No sauce or dip accompaniment is recommended for these buns.

Note: These buns may be frozen after cooking. They will keep 2 to 3 months. To reheat, defrost thoroughly and allow to come to room temperature. Then steam for 3 minutes, or until hot.

Steamed Vegetable Buns

So Choi Bau

I don't believe you will ever find these buns in a dim sum teahouse. They are my recipe, proof of the versatility and adaptability of the dim sum kitchen, wherein vegetables replace meats or sweets.

3 ounces cabbage (cut into 2-inch pieces, then shredded)
3 cups cold water
1/2 teaspoon salt
1/4 teaspoon baking soda

Sauce Ingredients

1 1/2 tablespoons oyster sauce
1/2 teaspoon light soy sauce
1/4 teaspoon dark soy sauce
1 teaspoon sesame oil
1 teaspoon Shao-Hsing wine or sherry
1/2 teaspoon sugar
Pinch white pepper
2 1/2 teaspoons tapioca flour
3 tablespoons cold water

To Continue Recipe

1 slice ginger, 1/2 inch thick, lightly smashed
1 teaspoon peanut oil
1 teaspoon minced ginger
1 scallion, finely sliced
1 soybean cake, cut into 3 pieces, then sliced across, thinly
3 Chinese black mushrooms, steamed (page 166), thinly sliced
1 teaspoon Shao-Hsing wine or sherry

Makes 8 buns

1. Mix the sauce ingredients. Reserve.
2. Water blanch the cabbage: In a pot place the 3 cups cold water, salt, baking soda, and slice of ginger. Bring to a boil over high heat. Add cabbage, making certain it is immersed, then stir.

Allow to cook for 1 minute or until tender. Turn off heat. Run cold water into pot. Drain. Set aside cabbage.

3. Heat wok over high heat for 30 seconds. Add 1 teaspoon of peanut oil and coat wok with spatula. When a wisp of white smoke appears add minced ginger. Stir. Add scallions. Stir. Cook for 30 seconds and add soybean cake. Stir and mix well. Add mushrooms and cabbage and combine thoroughly. Add wine and mix in. Cook for 1 minute. Make a well in the center of the mixture, stir sauce and pour in. Stir together until sauce thickens. Turn off heat. Transfer to a shallow dish, allow to come to room temperature then refrigerate overnight, uncovered.

4. Prepare buns: Follow procedures precisely as in recipe for Steamed Pork Buns (page 118).

Serving Suggestion: I do not recommend any sauce or dip with these buns.

Note: These vegetable buns cannot be frozen. They will keep 2 days refrigerated.

Lin Yung Bau

Steamed Lotus Seed Buns

This sweet bun is quite popular among Buddhist monks and nuns. These religious vegetarians, who like their buns but are precluded from eating those filled with meats or shrimp—as most dim sum dumplings are—eat these. At one time, because of the enormous amount of preparation time needed to prepare the lotus seed filling, these buns were rare and dear. These days the filling is available in cans and is quite good. There is no need to go through the trouble to prepare the filling to enjoy these buns.

1 can lotus seed paste
1 Steamed Bun Dough recipe (page 117)

Makes 8 buns

1. Remove the paste from its can and have it on hand. Cut parchment paper (or waxed paper) into eight 2½-inch squares.
2. Using Steamed Bun Dough recipe, roll dough into a sausage shape 8 inches long. Divide into 8 one-inch pieces. Work with one piece at a time, keeping others under a damp cloth. Roll each piece into a ball, then with your fingers, press to create a dome and a well.
3. Place 2 teaspoons of lotus seed paste filling into well. Hold bun in one hand and with the other turn the bun, pinching it closed. Press firmly to seal. (As your proficiency grows increase filling to 1 tablespoon.) Place completed bun, sealed side down, on a square of paper. Repeat until all buns are made. These should resemble baked pork buns.

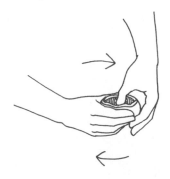

4. Place buns in a steamer at least 2 inches apart to allow for expansion. Steam for 15 to 20 minutes. Serve immediately.

Serving Suggestion: I recommend no accompaniment with these buns. Their sweetness is sufficient.

Note: These buns may be frozen after cooking. They will keep 2 to 3 months. To reheat, defrost thoroughly and allow to come to room temperature. Then steam for 3 minutes, or until hot.

Note: The lotus seed paste, kept in a closed plastic container, refrigerated, will keep 4 to 5 months.

Baked Bun Dough

Guk Bau
Min Teun

This dough is the basis for several of the best-known dim sum preparations outside of China. These are made with different fillings, then baked, which is why they are favored in the West. The concept of baking came late to China; most breads and cakes were steamed. As you may see, this is a simple dough, but it bakes beautifully.

1½   teaspoons dry yeast
5   tablespoons sugar
⅓   cup hot water
1⅓   cups high-gluten flour (Pillsbury Best Bread
Flour, enriched, bromide preferred)
1   small egg, beaten
3¾   tablespoons peanut oil

1. In a large mixing bowl, dissolve the yeast and sugar in hot water. Set in a warm place for 30 to 60 minutes, depending upon the outside temperature. (In winter the longer time will be required.)

2. When yeast rises and a brownish foam forms on top, add flour, egg, and peanut oil, stirring continuously with your hand. Begin kneading. When the mass becomes cohesive, sprinkle a work surface with flour, place dough on it, and continue kneading. Knead for about 15 minutes, picking up dough with a scraper and sprinkling the work surface with flour to prevent sticking.

3. When smooth and elastic, place dough in a large bowl. Cover the bowl with a damp cloth and put it in a warm place to rise. Dough will take from 2 to 4 hours to rise, depending upon temperature (it will take longer in cold weather). The dough is ready when it has tripled in size.

Note: This dough will perform better if made the night before, and is used the following day.

Baked Pork Buns

Guk Char
Siu Bau

焗
义
烧
館

To most non-Chinese, this is the most famous dish of the dim sum teahouse. People who are not familiar with the term dim sum know pork buns, and they are eaten daily by the thousands. I have experimented successfully with different fillings for these baked buns, but this is the bun of tradition.

Sauce Ingredients

- 2 **teaspoons oyster sauce**
- ³/₄ **teaspoon dark soy sauce**
- 2 **teaspoons ketchup**
- 1¹/₂ **teaspoons sugar**
  Pinch of white pepper
- 3 **tablespoons Chicken Broth (page 33)**
- ¹/₂ **teaspoon sesame oil**

To Continue Recipe

- 2 **teaspoons peanut oil**
- ¹/₃ **cup onions, cut into ¹/₄-inch dice**
- ¹/₂ **cup Roast Pork (page 121)**
- 1 **teaspoon Shao-Hsing wine or sherry**
- 1 **Baked Bun Dough recipe (page 132)**
- 1 **small egg, beaten**
- 2 **tablespoons Scallion Oil (page 36)**

Makes 8 buns

1. Combine the sauce ingredients. Reserve.
2. Prepare filling: Heat wok for 30 seconds over high heat. Add peanut oil and coat wok with spatula. When a wisp of white smoke appears, add onions, lower heat to low, and cook, turning occasionally, until onions turn light brown, 3 to 4 minutes. Add roast pork, raise heat, and stir-fry to combine the pork with the onions, about 1 minute. Add Shao-Hsing wine and mix well.
3. Lower heat, stir sauce mixture, and add to pork and onions. Stir until well mixed and sauce thickens and bubbles. Turn heat off. Remove mixture from wok and transfer to a shallow dish.

Allow to cool to room temperature, then refrigerate for 4 hours, uncovered, or overnight, covered.

4. Prepare Buns: Preheat over to 350°F. Cut 8 squares of waxed paper, 3½ inches on a side.

5. Remove reserved dough from bowl, knead several times, then roll it out with your hands into a sausage shape 8 inches long. Divide into 8 one-inch pieces. Work with one piece at a time, keeping others under a damp cloth.

6. Roll each piece into a ball, then with your fingers, press to create a dome and a well.

7. Place 2 teaspoons of pork filling into well. Hold bun in one hand and with the other turn the bun, pinching it closed. Press firmly to seal. (As your proficiency grows increase filling to 1 tablespoon.) Place completed bun, sealed side down, on a square of waxed paper. Repeat until all buns are made.

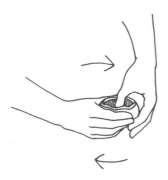

8. Place all buns on a cookie sheet, at least 2 inches apart, to allow for expansion. Put buns in a warm place for about 1 hour to permit them to rise. (The rising time will be longer in winter.) Using an atomizer, spray each bun lightly with warm water. With a pastry brush, brush each bun with beaten egg.

9. Bake for 15 to 20 minutes. Halfway through the baking time reverse the tray in oven. When buns are golden brown, remove then from the oven, and while still warm brush them with Scallion Oil. (As the buns cool, the crust tends to slightly harden.

The brushing with Scallion Oil prevents hardening, as well as adding piquancy.) Serve immediately.

Serving Suggestion: I suggest that these buns be eaten with no accompaniment. My husband likes them with a mixture of Hot Mustard (page 41) and chili sauce.

Note: I prefer these not be frozen. They will keep refrigerated for 3 to 4 days. When reheating, allow to come to room temperature, sprinkle lightly with water and heat in a 350°F oven for 5 minutes.

Baked Curry Pork Buns

焗生肉飽

Guk San
Yuk Bau

This recipe is a modern rendition of the marvelous Steamed Curried Pork Buns, created by Chun Wing, discussed earlier. His filling is as tasty in a baked bun as it is in a steamed one. I expect Chef Chun would like this very much.

¹/₄ **pound pork fillet**

Pork Marinade

³/₄ **teaspoon sesame oil**
¹/₂ **teaspoon light soy sauce**
¹/₄ **teaspoon dark soy sauce**
³/₄ **teaspoon sugar**
¹/₄ **teaspoon salt**
1 **teaspoon oyster sauce**
1 **teaspoon Shao-Hsing wine or sherry**
1 **teaspoon cornstarch**
Pinch of white pepper

Curry Paste

4 **teaspoons curry powder (Madras brand preferred) combined with**
2 **tablespoons Chicken Broth (page 33)**

Sauce Ingredients

2 **teaspoons oyster sauce**
2 **teaspoons cornstarch**
¹/₄ **cup Chicken Broth (page 33)**

To Continue Recipe

2¹/₂ **tablespoons peanut oil**
¹/₂ **cup onions, cut into ¹/₄-inch dice**
¹/₄ **cup sweet red peppers, cut into ¹/₄-inch dice**
1 **teaspoon minced ginger**
2 **tablespoons chopped fresh coriander**
1 **teaspoon minced garlic**
1 **Baked Bun Dough recipe (page 132)**
1 **small egg, beaten**
2 **tablespoons Scallion Oil (page 36)**

Makes 8 buns

1. Prepare filling: Cut pork fillets into pieces $1/2$ inch square, thinly sliced. Combine the marinade ingredients and marinate the pork. Reserve. Combine the curry paste ingredients and reserve. Combine the sauce ingredients and reserve.

2. Heat wok over high heat for 30 seconds. Add 1 tablespoon of peanut oil and coat wok with spatula. When a wisp of white smoke appears add the diced onions, lower heat to medium and stir and cook for 2 minutes until onions become translucent. Turn heat back to high, add the peppers, and stir-fry for 1 minute. Turn off heat. Remove onion and pepper mixture. Reserve. Wash and dry wok and spatula.

3. Heat wok over high heat for 30 seconds. Add remaining peanut oil and coat wok with spatula. When a wisp of white smoke appears add minced ginger. Stir. Add coriander and garlic and stir together. When garlic turns light brown add the curry paste and mix well. Cook for 1 minute until the curry aroma is released. Add pork and marinade. Spread in a thin layer and cook for 1 minute. Turn pork over and mix well. Add reserved onion and pepper mixture and stir together for 1 minute. Stir the sauce, make a well in the center of the mixture, add sauce. Mix all together, cooking for 2 minutes, or until the sauce thickens. Turn off heat. Transfer to a shallow dish and allow to cool to room temperature. Refrigerate for 4 hours, uncovered, or overnight, covered.

4. Prepare buns: Follow procedures precisely as in recipe for Baked Pork Buns (pages 133–35).

Serving Suggestion: No accompaniment is recommended, or needed, because of the curry taste.

Note: These should not be frozen. They will keep refrigerated for 3 or 4 days. When reheating, allow to come to room temperature, sprinkle lightly with water, and heat in a 350°F oven for 5 minutes.

Baked Chicken Buns

Guk Gai Bau

Baked buns traditionally are filled with roast pork, as we have seen. Here is my variation: I use stir-fried and seasoned chicken for the filling. My family is as enthusiastic about these as they are about baked buns filled with roast pork.

$^{1}/_{4}$ **pound skinless, boneless chicken breast, cut into $^{1}/_{3}$-inch cubes**

Marinade for Chicken

$^{1}/_{4}$ **teaspoon grated ginger mixed with $^{1}/_{2}$ teaspoon Shao-Hsing wine or sherry**

1 **teaspoon light soy sauce**

$^{1}/_{2}$ **teaspoon sesame oil**

$^{1}/_{2}$ **teaspoon sugar**

1$^{1}/_{2}$ **teaspoons oyster sauce**

Pinch of white pepper

$^{3}/_{4}$ **teaspoon cornstarch**

Sauce Ingredients

1 **tablespoon oyster sauce**

$^{1}/_{4}$ **teaspoon light soy sauce**

$^{1}/_{4}$ **teaspoon dark soy sauce**

$^{1}/_{2}$ **teaspoon sesame oil**

$^{1}/_{2}$ **teaspoon sugar**

$^{1}/_{8}$ **teaspoon salt**

2 **teaspoons cornstarch**

Pinch of white pepper

3 **tablespoons Chicken Broth (page 33)**

To Continue Recipe

1 **tablespoon peanut oil**

$^{1}/_{4}$ **cup Chinese black mushrooms, soaked in warm water for 30 minutes, cut into $^{1}/_{4}$-inch pieces**

1 **tablespoon bamboo shoots, cut into $^{1}/_{4}$-inch pieces**

1½ teaspoons Shao-Hsing wine or sherry
1 large scallion, white portion, minced
   (⅛ cup)
1 Baked Bun Dough recipe (page 132)
1 small egg, beaten
2 tablespoons Scallion Oil (page 36)

Makes 8 buns

1. Prepare filling: Combine the marinade ingredients and marinate chicken for 30 minutes. Reserve. Combine the sauce ingredients, reserve.

2. Heat wok over high heat for 30 seconds. Add 1 tablespoon peanut oil and coat wok with spatula. When a wisp of white smoke appears add chicken and the marinade. Spread in a thin layer, cook for 30 seconds. Turn over and mix. Add mushrooms, bamboo shoots, stir, and cook for 1 minute. Add wine. Mix well. Add scallions and cook together for 30 seconds. Make a well in the center of mixture, stir sauce, and pour in. Mix thoroughly until sauce thickens and bubbles. Turn off heat. Transfer to a shallow dish and allow to come to room temperature. Refrigerate for 4 hours, uncovered, or overnight, covered.

3. Prepare buns: Follow procedures precisely as in recipe for Baked Pork Buns (pages 133–35).

Serving Suggestion: These should be accompanied by Vinegar Ginger Dip (page 45).

Note: These buns should not be frozen. They will keep refrigerated for 3 or 4 days. When reheating, allow to come to room temperature, sprinkle lightly with water, and heat in a 350°F oven for 5 minutes.

Chapter 6

Some Regional Classics

The regions of China come together in the dim sum kitchen. Though most dim sum dumplings have their origins in Canton, other regions of China, particularly Shanghai as we have seen, have developed their own dumplings. Those famous potstickers, for example, are as familiar in the restaurants of Chengdu as they are in Shanghai, and many of Shanghai's other contributions to the dim sum kitchen have made their way to Beijing. Today the dim sum teahouse is no longer confined to Canton and the south of China, although it is at its most creative in Canton.

This section of the book has been set aside for some dim sum classics of various kinds that embody years of tradition in Canton and other parts of China where development came later. All are nevertheless entrenched in the dim sum repertoire. People return from China these days with tales of marvelous dim sum brunches not only in Hong Kong and Canton, but in Shanghai, Beijing, and Taiwan as well, and even in Szechuan and Hunan.

Jun Jiu Kau

Pearl Balls

This is a beautiful-looking dumpling. After the pearl balls are steamed, the kernels of glutinous rice adhering to them do indeed resemble tiny seed pearls. This is a Shanghai dumpling, and in Beijing you might find it as a first course in a banquet. You will notice directions in this recipe, and others in this book, to mix ingredients in one direction. This is both a personal tradition and a good kitchen technique. My grandmother told me always to mix in one direction or my ingredients would fall apart, and she happens to be right.

1 cup glutinous rice
1 pound lean ground pork
4 fresh water chestnuts, peeled, cut into
    $^1/_8$-inch dice
2 scallions, ends discarded, finely sliced
2 teaspoons minced ginger
1 large egg, beaten
1$^1/_2$ tablespoons cornstarch mixed with 2 table-
    spoons cold water
1$^1/_4$ teaspoons salt
2$^1/_2$ teaspoons sugar
1 teaspoon sesame oil
2 teaspoons light soy sauce
1$^1/_2$ teaspoons Shao-Hsing wine or sherry
    Pinch of white pepper
2 tablespoons Scallion Oil (page 36)
    Vegetable leaves

Makes 20 dumplings

1. Wash the rice and, in a bowl, soak it for 1 hour. Drain. In a strainer dry the rice for 2 hours. Reserve.

2. In a bowl combine all ingredients except rice. Mix in one direction with wooden spoon or 2 pairs of chopsticks until it becomes soft and well-blended, and all ingredients stick together. Refrigerate for 2 hours, uncovered.

3. Pick up a handful of the mixture, move it around in your hand gently, then squeeze. The amount that oozes through the top of the hand will be a ball about 1 inch in diameter. Repeat for rest of mixture.

4. Place all the balls on a sheet of waxed paper. On a second sheet of waxed paper smooth the dried rice into a thin layer.
5. Roll each ball through the rice so it receives a single coating of kernels.
6. Line a steamer with vegetable leaves. Place pearl balls on leaves and steam for 15 to 20 minutes, or until the rice becomes translucent and pork cooks through. Serve immediately.

Serving Suggestion: I recommend these be eaten with Garlic Pepper Sauce (page 40).

Note: These pearl balls cannot be frozen.

Chau Mai Ngau
Yuk Yeun

Dry-Roasted Rice Meatballs

This is a dim sum that must be credited, at least philosophically, to Szechuan Province. It is my creation, an adaptation of a Szechuan recipe. The Szechuanese use chunks of meat and coat them with dry-roasted crushed rice before steaming them. I do not fancy the taste that much. I have made small, seasoned beef meatballs, coated them with roasted crushed rice, and steamed them. They are one of my contributions to the dim sum repertoire.

  1 **cup white rice**
  1 **pound lean ground beef**
  4 **water chestnuts, peeled, diced**
  3 **scallions, ends discarded, finely sliced**
  1 **tablespoon minced ginger**
  1 **egg, beaten**
 1½ **tablespoons cornstarch mixed with 2 table-**
     spoons cold water
 1¼ **teaspoons salt**
 2½ **teaspoons sugar**
 1½ **teaspoons sesame oil**
 1½ **teaspoons light soy sauce**
  1 **teaspoon blended whiskey (or sherry or**
     cognac)
  2 **tablespoons Garlic Oil (page 39)**
     Pinch of white pepper
     Vegetable leaves

Makes 20 dumplings

1. Wash and soak rice for 1 hour. Drain and dry thoroughly. In a wok dry-roast the rice over medium heat for 5 to 7 minutes or until it is golden brown. When the rice cools, layer it onto a sheet of waxed paper. With a rolling pin, roll over the rice until it becomes coarse crumbs but is not powdery. Set aside on the sheet of waxed paper.

2. In a bowl combine all ingredients except rice and vegetable leaves. Mix in one direction with wooden spoon or 2 pairs of

chopsticks until it becomes soft and well-blended, and all ingredients stick together. Refrigerate 2 hours, uncovered.

3. Pick up a handful of the mixture, move it around in your hand gently, then squeeze. The amount that oozes through the top of the hand will be a ball about 1 inch in diameter. Repeat for rest of mixture.
4. Place ball on waxed paper. Repeat until all of the mixture has been used. Roll each meatball in the rice until it is thickly coated. Repeat until all meatballs are coated.
5. Place balls on a heatproof dish, then steam them for 5 to 7 minutes. These may also be steamed right in the steamer, but the bottom must first be lined with a layer of vegetable leaves to prevent sticking. Serve immediately.

Serving Suggestion: I recommend these be eaten with Garlic Pepper Sauce (page 40).

Note: These dry-roasted rice meatballs cannot be frozen.

Spare Ribs *Siu Mai*

Pai Gwat
Siu Mai

Is there anyone who does not adore Chinese-style spare ribs? Not likely. Nor can a Cantonese restaurant be found that doesn't have spare ribs on the menu. But not these spare ribs. Dim sum spare ribs are neither barbecued, roasted, nor broiled, but are steamed with black beans. This is one of the oldest dim sum treats. Its name is confusing, because it bears the same name as the Cook and Sell Dumplings (page 66). But Pai Gwat Siu Mai has always been a Siu Mai and that is what it will remain.

2¹/₂ **pounds pork spare ribs (net weight after cutting and trimming; have the butcher cut ribs *across* the bones at 1¹/₂-inch intervals)**

Marinade Ingredients

2 **teaspoons salt**

2 **tablespoons sugar**

1 **tablespoon Shao-Hsing wine or sherry**

2 **tablespoons oyster sauce**

1 **teaspoon sesame oil**

2 **teaspoons minced garlic**

2 **tablespoons fermented black beans, washed**

¹/₄ **teaspoon baking soda**

4 **tablespoons tapioca flour**

Pinch of white pepper

¹/₂ **teaspoon dried hot pepper flakes, or 1 tablespoon of fresh hot pepper, minced**

2 **tablespoons fresh red bell peppers, sliced**

Makes 3 cups of ribs

1. Trim spare ribs, making certain you have 1¹/₂-inch pieces.
2. Combine the marinade ingredients except bell peppers. Add spare rib pieces, mix thoroughly, and refrigerate overnight.
3. Place the spare ribs and the marinade in a heatproof dish and steam for 30 minutes, or until done.

4. Place spare ribs in a serving dish, garnish with red pepper slices, and serve immediately.

Serving Suggestion: I recommend no acccompaniment for spare ribs.

Note: Depending upon the size of racks of ribs, you will have between 24 and 30 spare rib pieces. This will serve 6 people as dim sum.

Note: Spare ribs can be frozen. To heat up, allow to defrost to room temperature, then steam for 8 to 10 minutes, or until hot.

Taro Root Horns

Woo Gok

Taro root is a traditional food during the Festival of the August Moon, when it is served plain after being boiled. At New Year's it is made into cakes or finely sliced and fried as chips, similar to potato chips. At other times of the year it is made into dim sum—the fluffy, egg-shaped Woo Gok—after being steamed and mashed. I have a particular fondness for Woo Gok because I introduced my husband to it when we first met in Hong Kong. It became his favorite dim sum dumpling during our honeymoon, and after.

3 ounces fresh shrimp, shelled, washed, dried, deveined, cut into 1/8-inch dice

3 ounces fresh lean pork, cut into 1/8-inch dice

2 medium Chinese black mushrooms, soaked in hot water for 30 minutes, squeezed, stems removed, cut into 1/8-inch dice

Marinade Ingredients

1/4 teaspoon salt

3/4 teaspoon sugar

1/2 teaspoon light soy sauce

1/2 teaspoon sesame oil

2 tablespoons oyster sauce

1 teaspoon Shao-Hsing wine or sherry

Pinch of white pepper

1/2 tablespoon cornstarch

Taro Root Dough Ingredients

1 pound of taro root, to yield 3/4 pound of cooked, mashed taro (see note)

1/3 cup wheat starch

1/2 cup plus 2 tablespoons boiling water (5 ounces)

1/2 teaspoon salt

1 teaspoon five-spice powder

1/3 cup peanut oil

To Finish the Dish

1 1/2 tablespoons peanut oil (for stir-frying filling)

5 cups peanut oil (for deep-frying)

Makes 16 dumplings

1. Combine the marinade ingredients. Add pork, shrimp, and mushrooms and marinate for 30 minutes. Reserve.

2. Heat wok over high heat for 30 seconds. Add 1½ tablespoons peanut oil and coat wok with spatula. When a wisp of white smoke appears add filling mixture and marinade. Spread in a thin layer and cook for 1 minute. Turn over and mix. Cook until pork and shrimp change color, about 1 more minute. Turn off heat. Transfer to a shallow dish and refrigerate for 4 hours, uncovered, or overnight, covered. This filling is to be used chilled.

3. Prepare taro root dough: Peel the taro, cut into large pieces, and steam for 1 hour. To make certain the pieces are tender, insert a chopstick into a piece of the taro. If it goes in easily, the taro root is cooked. Allow to cool a bit, then mash the taro root with your fingers. It should be quite smooth.

   In a large mixing bowl, mix wheat starch with boiling water. As you pour the water, simultaneously stir the mixture with chopsticks. Stir until mixture becomes a paste. Add the mashed taro to the paste. Add salt, five-spice powder, and ⅓ cup peanut oil. Knead like a dough until all ingredients are well blended.

4. Make the dumpling: Place 1 tablespoon of chilled filling in the center of the well; then, holding *Woo Gok* in one hand, thumb in the middle, turn and close with the other hand. When hole is closed, gently shape the dumpling into an oval. Repeat until all the dough mixture and filling are used.

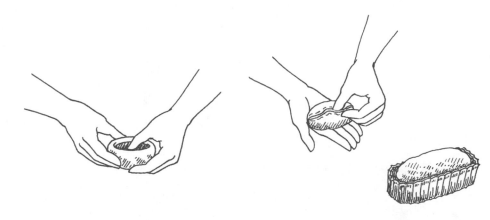

5. Heat the 5 cups of peanut oil in wok to 350°F to 375°F. Place dumplings, 4 at a time, in wok and deep-fry until golden brown on both sides, 3 to 4 minutes. Drain on paper towels. Serve immediately in fluted paper cups, which can be purchased at any supermarket or food store.

Serving Suggestion: I recommend these be eaten with dabs of Hot Mustard (page 41) or with mustard combined with Chinese chili paste.

Note: *Woo Gok* cannot be frozen, but can be prepared a day ahead, which I recommend. To reheat, after they have been fried, deep-fry for 1 to 2 minutes to heat through.

Note: The best taro root is threaded with delicate purple thread-like veins. Ask your grocer for this sort of root because it has a fine fragrance and cooks and tastes better.

Vegetarian Taro Horns

So Woo Gok

In Canton this version of Woo Gok *is made both for those who are religious and do not eat meat or shrimp, and for others who wish a touch of variety. This vegetarian dumpling is quite popular, particularly at New Year's, because one can eat a favored dumpling and still not violate Buddhist tradition. It is sort of like having your dumpling and eating it too.*

Sauce Ingredients	
1¹/₂	tablespoons oyster sauce
1	teaspoon sesame oil
1	teaspoon sugar
1	teaspoon Shao-Hsing wine or sherry
1	teaspoon light soy sauce
2¹/₂	teaspoons tapioca flour
	Pinch of white pepper
4	tablespoons cold water

To Continue Recipe

1 tablespoon Garlic Oil (page 39)

¹/₈ teaspoon salt

¹/₄ pound snow peas, both ends and strings removed, cut into ¹/₄-inch pieces (1 cup)

2 scallions, both ends removed, finely sliced (¹/₂ cup)

3 Chinese black mushrooms, steamed (page 166), cut into ¹/₈-inch pieces (¹/₃ cup)

1 Taro Root Dough preparation (see Taro Root Horns, page 148)

Makes 16 dumplings

1. Mix sauce ingredients. Reserve.
2. Prepare filling: Heat wok over high heat for 30 seconds. Add garlic oil and coat wok with spatula. Add salt. When a wisp of white smoke appears, add snow peas and scallions. Stir and cook for 30 seconds. Add mushrooms, stir, and cook for 1 minute more. Stir sauce, make a well in the center of the mixture, and pour in. Stir and mix well. When sauce thickens,

turn off heat. Transfer to a shallow dish. Allow to come to room temperature, then refrigerate for 4 hours, uncovered, or overnight, covered.

3. Make the dumplings: Using the Taro Root Dough (page 148), make the *Woo Gok* precisely in the same manner as in the recipe for Taro Root Horns, and deep-fry identically.

Serving Suggestion: I recommend these be eaten with Hot Mustard (page 41) or with mustard combined with Chinese chili paste.

Note: Vegetarian *Woo Gok* cannot be frozen, but can be prepared a day ahead, which I recommend. After cooking, the *Woo Gok* can be reheated by deep-frying for 1 to 2 minutes to heat through.

Yunnan Ham Roll

Wan Tui Geun

This dim sum is a three-province blend. It incorporates the strong cured ham of Yunnan, the most highly prized in all of China, the crisp cabbage of Tientsin, and the cooking tradition of the Cantonese dim sum teahouse. Yunnan ham is unavailable in the United States, so I substitute Smithfield ham from Virginia, and this American ham is a fine substitute indeed.

- $^1\!/_4$ pound Smithfield ham
- 6 cups cold water
- $^1\!/_2$ pound shrimp, shelled, deveined, washed, dried, cut into $^1\!/_4$-inch dice
- $1^1\!/_2$ tablespoons Scallion Oil (page 36)
- $^3\!/_4$ teaspoon salt
- $1^1\!/_2$ teaspoons sugar
- $^1\!/_4$ pound lean ground pork
- $1^1\!/_2$ teaspoons light soy sauce
- $^1\!/_2$ teaspoon sesame oil
- 1 tablespoon oyster sauce
- 1 teaspoon grated fresh ginger mixed with 1 tablespoon of Shao-Hsing wine or sherry
- 1 tablespoon cornstarch
- 1 teaspoon finely chopped fresh coriander
- $^1\!/_4$ cup Chinese black mushrooms, steamed (page 166), cut into $^1\!/_8$-inch pieces
- $^1\!/_4$ cup bamboo shoots, cut into $^1\!/_8$-inch dice
- $^1\!/_2$ cup scallions, ends discarded, finely sliced
  Pinch of white pepper
- 10 stalked large-leafed Tientsin bok choy (or cabbage)
- 8 cups cold water
- 1 teaspoon baking soda
- $^1\!/_2$ carrot, peeled, cut into 2-inch sections, then into matchsticks

Makes 10 dumplings

1. Prepare the ham: In a pot, place 6 cups of cold water and the Smithfield ham. Turn heat to high, cover pot, and bring to a boil. Lower heat to medium/low, leave lid of pot open a crack, and allow ham to simmer for $1\frac{1}{2}$ hours. (This removes curing salt from ham.) Turn off heat. Pour off liquid from pot. Run cold water into pot and allow ham to cool in water, about 20 minutes. Remove, dry, and cut into 10 equal pieces.

2. As the ham boils, make the filling: Mix all other ingredients, except leaves and carrot, in a bowl. Stir together until well blended. Refrigerate, in a shallow dish, for 4 hours, uncovered, or overnight, covered.

3. Prepare the leaves: Remove leafy stalks, piece by piece, from the head of Tientsin bok choy, or cabbage. Wash and drain. Place 8 cups of water and 1 teaspoon of baking soda in a pot and bring to a boil. Place leaves in the water, cover with water, and allow to simmer for 2 minutes, or until softened. Remove leaves from boiling water and place them in a large bowl. Run the leaves under cold running water, drain, and pat dry with paper towels.

4. Make the dumplings: Lay a leaf stalk flat on the work surface. Place $3\frac{1}{2}$ tablespoons of the filling mixture onto the leaf. On top of the mixture place 1 piece of Smithfield ham and a piece of carrot. Roll toward the leafy end of the stalk, folding in edges as you do, to create a packet. Repeat until you have made all dumplings.

5. Steam the dumplings for 15 to 20 minutes. Remove from steamer and serve immediately.

Serving Suggestion: These dumplings are complemented well by Vinegar Ginger Dip (page 45).

Note: These dumplings cannot be frozen.

Chapter 7

The Ubiquitous Shrimp

By now, you surely will have noted the extensive use of shrimp as a dumpling ingredient. In the Cantonese dialect, the word for shrimp is *har*, which is also the word for the sound of laughter. Shrimp is regarded as a most delightful food and is used in a variety of ways—as a main ingredient, as an accompaniment, and often as a subtle flavoring. No banquets and few Cantonese meals, dim sum or otherwise, are considered complete until the shrimp appears in some form.

The widespread use of shrimp also reflects its availability. Shrimp, in all of its variations, abounds in the fresh- and saltwater of China. Where I lived as a girl, in Sun Tak, outside of Canton, we would pick up shrimp right out of the streams. We had an abundance of sweet freshwater shrimp, which we ate in many ways including in dim sum dumplings. I can even remember eating tiny shrimp that had first been boiled, then dried in the sun, as a sweet snack.

This chapter is devoted to shrimp as a primary filling for dim sum, not in combination with anything else. Using a basic shrimp filling—truly a classic recipe—you will be able to experience the compatibility of shrimp with other foods that encase the filling. Also included is shrimp toast, a favorite dim sum.

Har Hom

Basic Shrimp Filling

This is a classic filling used in a variety of teahouse dim sum. When thoroughly blended and allowed to stand, it acquires an elegant and delicate taste that complements other foods perfectly. It can be served as an hors d'oeuvre or as a first course.

> 1 pound shrimp, shelled, deveined, washed, dried, and quartered (yielding 14 ounces)
> $^3/_4$ teaspoon salt
> $^1/_2$ teaspoon sugar
> $^1/_4$ cup bamboo shoots, cut into $^1/_8$-inch dice
> 2 scallions, ends discarded, finely sliced
> 1 egg white, beaten
> 2 teaspoons oyster sauce
> 1 teaspoon sesame oil
> 1 teaspoon Shao-Hsing wine or sherry
>   Pinch of white pepper

1. Place shrimp and all other ingredients in a large mixing bowl and mix, in one direction, with a wooden spoon or 2 pairs of chopsticks, for about 5 minutes until well blended.

2. Place mixture in a shallow dish and refrigerate for at least 4 hours. (It is much easier to stuff dim sum when the mixture is cold.) When thoroughly chilled, use in the recipes that call for it.

Yung Hai Kim

Stuffed Crab Claws

Although these are called "stuffed" crab claws, they are actually croquettes molded around the outside of crab claws. The crab claws can be purchased at any fish market.

1   **Basic Shrimp Filling recipe (page 158)**
8   **crab claws, medium, hard-shelled (see note)**
2   **tablespoons plus ½ cup tapioca flour, for dusting**
5   **cups peanut oil**

Makes 8 crab claws

1. Prepare Basic Shrimp Filling. Make certain it is thoroughly chilled.
2. Steam crab claws for 5 minutes. Reserve.
3. Sprinkle surface of a cookie sheet with the 2 tablespoons tapioca flour, covering completely. In a shallow dish place the ½ cup of tapioca flour.
4. Take a handful of the filling and, with an opening-closing motion of the hand, smooth the filling into a ball. Then make a fist and remove excess filling as it oozes out over the thumb. You will have a ball 1½ inches in diameter. Place the balls on the floured cookie sheet.

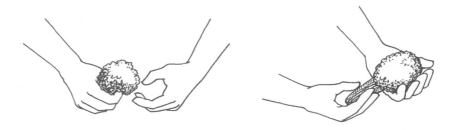

5. Press a crab claw, meat side down, into the center of each ball of filling. Coat your hands with tapioca flour from the bowl; lift crab claw and filling with both hands and pack filling gently

around the claw, dusting with tapioca flour as you do so. Gently pack filling against the claw with one hand, turning it with the other. Seal the filling around the claw with your little finger. Continue until a smooth, croquette-shaped covering is achieved. Repeat until all crab claws are prepared.

6. Heat the peanut oil in a wok to 350°F to 375°F. Place 1 batch of 4 crab claws in the oil and fry until golden brown, 3 to 4 minutes. Repeat with second batch. Serve immediately.

Serving Suggestion: I prefer to eat these without accompaniment, but a few drops of Hot Oil (page 37) go quite well with the claws.

Note: The crab claws can be frozen after frying for up to a month. To reheat, allow to come to room temperature, then either fry lightly in peanut oil or warm them in a preheated 350°F oven, until hot.

Note: Crab claws usually come with half of the shells removed across the palm of the claw. If they are not so prepared, ask your fishmonger to cut the shells for you.

Har Yeun

Shrimp Balls

This simple dim sum is very popular. In the teahouse you will receive them if you ask for har yeun, *which translates as "shrimp round," or* har kau, *which means "shrimp ball." They are however the same. These shrimp balls are a teahouse dumpling that has made its way into the home kitchen with ease.*

> 1 **Basic Shrimp Filling recipe (page 158)**
> 2 **tablespoons tapioca flour, plus ¹/₂ cup tapioca flour, for dusting**
> 5 **cups peanut oil**

Makes 10 shrimp balls

1. Dust a cookie sheet with the 4 tablespoons of tapioca flour to cover completely. Pour ¹/₂ cup of tapioca flour into shallow bowl.
2. Dust your hands with the flour from the bowl and, with both hands, pick up a ball of filling. Gently form into a ball, coating with tapioca flour as you do so. Toss the ball from hand to hand, gently, allowing it to fall into the palm of each hand. This makes the shrimp ball firm. Place each finished ball onto the cookie sheet. Each ball should be about 1¹/₂ inches in diameter.
3. Heat oil to 325°F to 350°F. Before placing each ball into oil firm it up again. Deep-fry in two batches, until golden brown, 4 to 5 minutes. Drain and serve.

Serving Suggestion: When the shrimp balls are fried, I prefer no accompaniment with them. When they're steamed, I like Ginger Soy Sauce (page 38).

Note: These shrimp balls may also be steamed. Place them in a steamer lined with vegetable leaves and steam for 5 minutes.

Note: Shrimp balls may be frozen after cooking. They will keep 2 to 3 days in refrigerator. To reheat, allow to come to room temperature and deep-fry for 2 minutes. Or steam until hot, 3 to 4 minutes.

Stuffed Bean Curd

Yung Dau Fu

This dim sum weds two loves of the Chinese: shrimp and bean curd, which is eaten in all manner of preparations. Bean curd should always be purchased fresh and stored in a container of fresh water in the refrigerator. Bean curd will stay fresh for 2 to 3 weeks if the water is changed daily.

¹/₄ **Basic Shrimp Filling recipe (page 158)**
4 **cakes fresh bean curd**
    Tapioca flour for dusting
3 **tablespoons peanut oil**

Makes 8 stuffed cakes

1. Remove bean curd from water. Allow to drain through a strainer 3 to 4 hours. Pat dry thoroughly with a paper towel.
2. Cut each cake diagonally and, with a pointed knife, cut out a pocket in each of its halves, on the diagonal side. Dust the pocket with tapioca flour, then fill with 1 tablespoon of the filling. Pack smoothly with the knife or with your fingers.

3. Place the peanut oil in a cast iron frying pan. Heat over high heat until a wisp of white smoke appears. With the stuffed side of the bean curd down, pan-fry over medium heat for 6 minutes. Turn the cakes and fry the other side for 2 minutes each. Serve hot.

Sᴇʀᴠɪɴɢ Sᴜɢɢᴇꜱᴛɪᴏɴ: I prefer a bit of Hot Oil (page 37) with these.

Note: These may be steamed. Line a steamer with vegetable leaves. Place cakes, on their sides, in the steamer and steam until shrimp turns pink in color, about 8 minutes. When steamed, I prefer them with Ginger Soy Sauce (page 38).

They also may be deep-fried. Place 4 cups of peanut oil in a wok and heat to 325°F. Fry the cakes, in 2 batches, until golden brown, about 8 minutes. Drain and serve. With these I prefer Hot Mustard (page 41) or mustard mixed with Chinese chili paste.

Note: These cannot be frozen. They should be made fresh and eaten the same day.

百花燒賣

Bok Far
Siu Mai

Stuffed Mushrooms

These stuffed mushrooms are a most popular dim sum, one that is always available in the dim sum restaurants and teahouses, or can be quite easily made at home. To the Chinese, the mushroom, when it is to used to hold this shrimp filling, resembles a small, open flower. Thus its name, Bok Far, which translates as "a hundred flowers."

¹/₂ **Basic Shrimp Filling recipe (page 158)**
12 **Chinese black mushrooms, steamed (page 166)**
     Tapioca flour for dusting
     Vegetable leaves

Makes 12 stuffed mushrooms

1. In the cavity of each mushroom, sprinkle tapioca flour to bind the filling to the mushroom. Pack each mushroom with 1 to 1¹/₂ tablespoons of the filling. With your finger, smooth the filling and gently press it down to make certain it will not fall out.

2. Line a steamer with vegetable leaves. Place stuffed mushrooms, filled sides up, in the steamer. Steam 4 to 6 minutes or until the shrimp turns pink. Serve immediately.

Serving Suggestion: Because of the wonderful tastes of both mushrooms and fillings, I suggest that no accompaniment be used with these.

Note: The mushrooms also may be pan-fried, in 3 tablespoons peanut oil, in a cast iron skillet, until the filling and mushrooms brown, 3 minutes on the filled side, 2 minutes on the other.

Note: These stuffed mushrooms cannot be frozen. They will keep, after cooking, for 2 to 3 days in the refrigerator. To reheat, steam for 3 to 4 minutes, or pan-fry 2 to 3 minutes, until hot.

Jing Dong Go

Steamed Mushrooms

Steamed mushrooms appear frequently in this book, in large part because of their versatility. They may be eaten hot, directly after steaming, as a dish in their own right, or at room temperature, or cold. In China they are eaten in all of these ways, because they are quite tasty at any temperature. Restaurants use them widely, often as a first course to accompany cold meat dishes.

20 large Chinese black mushrooms
 1 slice fresh ginger, 1 inch thick, lightly smashed
 3 scallions, ends discarded, cut into 3-inch sections
 2 tablespoons Garlic Oil (page 39)
 1 teaspoon sesame oil
 1 tablespoon Shao-Hsing wine or sherry
 1 tablespoon dark soy sauce
 2 teaspoons sugar
 $1/2$ teaspoon salt
 $1/3$ cup Chicken Broth (page 33)

1. Soak the mushrooms in hot water for 1 hour, until they soften. Wash well and squeeze out excess water. Remove stems and place mushrooms in a bowl.

2. Combine all of the remaining ingredients in a large bowl, then pour over the mushrooms. Mix well to coat the mushrooms completely.

3. Place the mushrooms and their sauce in a heatproof dish and steam for 30 minutes. Turn off heat and allow to come to room temperature. The mushrooms are now ready for use.

Note: After steaming they may be refrigerated kept in a closed plastic container. They will keep for 10 days to 2 weeks. This makes them perfect for inclusion in the recipes in this book, for they can be prepared in advance and stored. They may not be frozen.

Note: The steaming liquid and its contents should not be discarded. They are fine additions to sauces and soups.

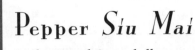

Pepper *Siu Mai*

Yeung Lah Chiu

In the United States bell peppers are used for this dim sum. In China, longer, somewhat hot, pointed peppers were always used. These were called ngau gok ju, *or "cows horns," because of their shape. If you wish to make the hot version, use those long, hot Italian red or green peppers.*

> 1 **medium red bell pepper**
> 1 **medium green bell pepper**
> **Tapioca flour for dusting**
> ¹/₂ **Basic Shrimp Filling recipe (page 158)**
> **Vegetable leaves**

Makes 16 stuffed peppers

1. Cut each pepper lengthwise into quarters, and remove seeds and membranes. Cut each quarter in half, across, making eight pieces, 16 pieces from both peppers. Trim each of these pieces along the cut edge, to make a square piece, about 1¹/₂ inches on a side. The curved ends of the pepper pieces must be retained, for they help secure the filling.

2. Sprinkle a bit of the tapioca flour into the cavity of each pepper piece, then pack about 1 tablespoon of shrimp filling into it with a knife or with your fingers.

3. Line a steamer with vegetable leaves. Place stuffed peppers, filled sides up, in the steamer. Steam for 5 to 7 minutes, until shrimp turns pink. Serve immediately.

Serving Suggestion: I recommend Sweet Scallion Sauce (page 37) with these, whether they are steamed or pan-fried.

Note: These stuffed peppers also may be pan-fried in 3 tablespoons of peanut oil, in a cast iron skillet, until the fillings and pepper brown, 3 minutes on the filled side, 2 minutes on the other.

Note: These stuffed peppers cannot be frozen. They will keep, after cooking, for 2 to 3 days in the refrigerator. To reheat, steam for 3 to 4 minutes, or pan-fry 2 to 3 minutes, until hot.

Shrimp Toast

Har Dor See

Cantonese chefs created this dim sum with its Western touch. The use of bread, and bread crumbs, not traditional foodstuffs in most of China, makes them unique. As you might expect, shrimp toast is a great favorite of both non-Chinese and Chinese people alike.

 6 ounces shrimp, shelled, deveined, washed, dried, chopped into a paste
 $^1/_2$ pound onions, cut into a very fine dice (see note)
 1 teaspoon grated ginger mixed with 1 teaspoon Shao-Hsing wine or sherry
 $^3/_4$ teaspoon salt
 $1^1/_4$ teaspoons sugar
 1 tablespoon sesame oil
 1 teaspoon oyster sauce
   Pinch of white pepper
 1 egg white
 2 tablespoons cornstarch
 4 slices firm white bread
 1 egg, beaten
 1 cup bread crumbs
 5 cups peanut oil

Makes 16 shrimp toasts

1. In a large bowl combine the shrimp, onions, and the grated ginger-wine mixture. Mix well, then immediately add salt, sugar, sesame oil, oyster sauce, white pepper, egg white, and cornstarch. With a wooden spoon or 2 pairs of chopsticks, stir in one direction until the mixture is thoroughly blended. Refrigerate for 3 hours, uncovered, or until it is completely chilled.

2. Trim the crusts from 4 slices of bread, then cut each of these slices diagonally to form 4 triangles. Allow the bread to stand at least 15 minutes, so that it begins to dry out.

3. Mound 1 tablespoon of the chilled filling onto a bread triangle. Using your fingers, seal the shrimp mixture with the beaten

egg. Cover the filling evenly with the bread crumbs and, with your fingers, pat and shape into a pyramid-like mound. Shake off any excess bread crumbs.

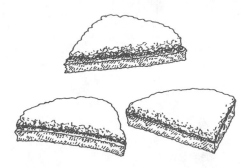

4. Deep-fry in the peanut oil at 325°F to 350°F, in three batches, 5 to 7 minutes, or until golden brown. Turn over frequently to ensure even browning. Serve immediately.

Serving Suggestion: My favorite accompaniment for these is Chinese chili paste or sauce.

Note: Shrimp toasts cannot be frozen. After cooking they may be refrigerated for 2 to 3 days. To reheat, either deep-fry them for 1 to 2 minutes, or warm them in a 350°F oven for 5 minutes, until hot.

Note: Try to use older, yellow onions as opposed to fresh ones. Younger onions contain a great deal of water and tend to make the shrimp toasts soggy.

Chapter 8

Spring Rolls:
A Seasonal Greeting

Spring rolls, in their many forms, are favorites in southeastern China, from Canton to Shanghai. The Cantonese words for spring roll are *chun geun*, and they are an element in the celebration of the season. Spring begins for the Chinese on New Year's Day, the first day of the lunar calendar.

Among the many special foods of the New Year is the spring roll, which is filled with scallions (often called spring onions), tender young bamboo shoots, and fresh water chestnuts, all indicative of spring and freshness. Yet they can be filled with other vegetables, meats, and seafood, as well. The spring roll is a most accommodating package. They are small and delicate when made correctly and are much favored as dim sum. More and more of these tasty fingerlike cylinders are to be seen in teahouses. People often refer to them generically as egg rolls, which is a misnomer. There are egg rolls in China, but they are not those big rolls we so often see in some restaurants and as snack foods. Rather, they are spring roll size, with skins just a bit thicker, and with shredded egg pancakes added to their filling.

This chapter provides a brief history of the spring roll, from its traditions to its classic forms, including the spring roll that was native to my childhood home. I have also included my version of a vegetable spring roll that is in the Buddhist tradition. I conclude with contemporary times and two original spring roll creations, and finally with my version of that wrapped food so dear to generations of Westerners, the American Egg Roll.

Chun Geun Pei

Spring Roll Skins

Here is the basis for the spring roll, as it is made in China. I would prefer that you buy the skins, because making them from scratch is a good deal of work. Nevertheless, if you do not have access to a Chinese or Asian grocery and if your market does not stock ready-made spring roll skins, or if you wish to have the satisfaction of making something that is truly an achievement, then make your own from scratch.

4¹/₂ cups bleached flour (Gold Medal All-
      Purpose, enriched, bleached preferred)
1¹/₂ teaspoons salt
2¹/₄ cups cold water

Makes about 40 skins

1. In a large mixing bowl, combine the flour and salt. Slowly add the water, using your fingers to mix the ingredients until they are well combined. Knead the dough by hand for about 20 minutes or until it becomes elastic. Cover the dough with a damp cloth and allow it to rest at room temperature for 3 to 4 hours. You can store the dough in the refrigerator overnight, but you must allow it to return to room temperature before you begin to make the skins.

2. Wash and dry a griddle. Make certain it is free of excess grease.

3. Place griddle over low heat. Grasp a large handful of dough from the bowl, hold it up, and rotate your wrist in a constant slow motion. Keep the dough held upward, working it with fingers and palm.

4. Quickly press the dough onto the center of the griddle, using a circular motion, reverse the motion once, then quickly pull back, leaving a thin layer of dough on the griddle.

5. The dough will start to dry on the edges in 10 to 12 seconds. Peel the skin from the griddle and put it on a large plate. After you have made 5 or 6 skins, wrap them in a damp cloth to prevent them from drying out. They are not ready for use.

Note: Skins must be prepared at least a day in advance of making spring rolls. To store, wrap them in a damp cloth, place the cloth-wrapped skins in a plastic bag, and refrigerate. Spring roll skins can be stored for up to 4 days or can be frozen for 1 to 2 months.

READY-MADE SPRING ROLL SKINS

Spring Roll Skins are available in a number of varieties and brands in Chinese and Asian groceries, and these days, even in some supermarkets. They come in either square or round shapes and carry several labels, described below.

"Egg Roll Skins" labels are found on packages of large, square skins, about 7 inches on a side. They come in either 1-pound or 2-pound packs, 7 skins to the pound, usually 15 to the 2-pound pack. These skins are somewhat thick and are sandy in color. They are recommended for the Surprise Package (page 188) and American Egg Roll (page 190) recipes.

"Shanghai Spring Roll" skins are found in the refrigerated compartments of markets. Unfortunately, they are rarely labeled in English, so you must ask for them by name. They come in 4-ounce (10 skins) and 8-ounce (20 skins) packages, either square or round. Squares are 7 inches on a side; round they are 7 inches in diameter. They are white in color, very thin, and may be used with all of the spring roll recipes, except the two noted above.

There are also those "Egg Roll Skins" that are not like the first thick kind, but are virtually identical to the Shanghai Spring Roll skins. They come packaged the same, 4-ounce (10 skins) or 8-ounce (20 skins) packages and are thin and white. They are also found in the refrigerated cases of markets. They are wrapped in sealed plastic bags, whereas the others (the first "Egg Roll Skins" discussed) are folded in wax paper and sealed with paper tape.

You may also see packages labeled "Spring Roll Shells." They are identical to the previous two. I am providing all of the names and descriptions because different manufacturers carry different labeling.

The major differences between the sandy colored egg roll skin and the white skins are as follows:

The sandy, often yellowish, thicker egg roll skin is a rolled dough, uncooked, made usually with eggs in the dough.

The thinner white skins have already been cooked on the griddle (see Spring Roll Skins, page 175) and contain no eggs. Any of these white skins are suitable for spring rolls.

In all of the recipes I specify the number of skins to be used. You may use either square or round skins for the recipes. However, when using a square skin, place the filling to be enclosed in a line across one corner of the skin before rolling. If using a round skin, place the filling across an edge closest to you, then roll.

Cantonese Spring Rolls

Guangdong
Chun Geun

This is the classic spring roll of the dim sum teahouse tradition. When you request spring rolls, these are what you will receive, although individual chefs change one or more of the ingredients according to the season, their whims, or the demands of customers. But this Cantonese Spring Roll is the original.

Sauce Ingredients

1 teaspoon light soy sauce
1 tablespoon oyster sauce
4 teaspoons cornstarch
¹/₈ teaspoon salt
³/₄ teaspoon sugar
Pinch of white pepper
¹/₄ cup Chicken Broth (page 33)

To Finish the Recipe

2 cups peanut oil (for blanching)
2 ounces fresh pork, shredded
6 shrimp, washed, shelled, deveined, quartered (2 ounces)
3 water chestnuts, peeled, julienned
³/₄ cup bamboo shoots, shredded
4 scallions, ends discarded, cut into 1¹/₂-inch pieces, white portions shredded
¹/₂ tablespoon Shao-Hsing wine or sherry
³/₄ teaspoon sesame oil
15 spring roll skins
1 egg, beaten
5 cups peanut oil (for deep-frying)

Makes 15 spring rolls

1. Combine the sauce ingredients and reserve.
2. Heat a wok over high heat for 40 seconds. Add the 2 cups of peanut oil and heat to 325°F. Blanch the filling: Place shredded pork in the hot oil, gently separating the shreds. Add the shrimp, also separating the pieces. Add water chestnuts, bamboo shoots, and scallions, and allow the ingredients to cook for 1 minute.

Remove from wok with a strainer and drain over a large bowl until the oil has drained from the filling. Occasionally loosen the filling to help drainage.

3. Remove oil from wok, leaving about 2 tablespoons. Heat wok over high heat for 30 seconds. Add filling ingredients from the strainer. Over very high heat stir-fry for 1 to 2 minutes, then add the wine around the edge of the wok. Mix thoroughly.

4. Make a well in the center. Stir sauce and pour in. Mix together quickly, stir-frying until the sauce thickens and bubbles. Turn off heat, add the sesame oil, and mix well. Remove from wok, place in a shallow dish, and allow to cool to room temperature. Refrigerate, uncovered, for 4 hours or overnight, covered.

5. Make the spring rolls: Spread out skin. Place 1½ tablespoons of the filling in a line, diagonally, at one end of the skin. Dip your fingers in the beaten egg and rub along the edges of the skin. Begin folding. Fold tip over filling, then continue to roll, folding in sides as you do. Keep rubbing the beaten egg along the edges as you fold to ensure that the spring roll will be sealed. Press and seal the end closed. Repeat until all spring rolls are made. All spring rolls are fashioned in this manner.

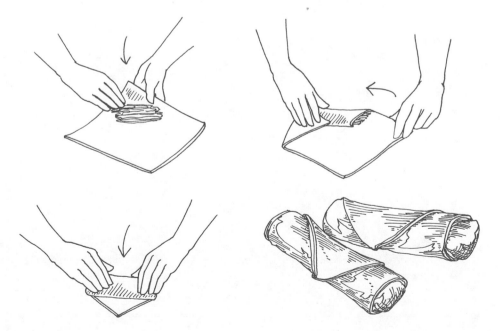

6. Deep-fry in 5 cups of peanut oil at 325°F (in 4 batches) until golden brown, 3 to 4 minutes. Keep turning spring rolls to ensure even color. Remove from oil, drain, and serve immediately.

Serving Suggestion: Vinegar Ginger Dip (page 45) is a fine accompaniment with these. Chinese chili sauce will do nicely as well.

Note: Cantonese Spring Rolls can be frozen after cooking. To reheat, either deep-fry lightly (at 325°F) for 1 minute, or heat in a preheated 375°F oven for 3 minutes on a side, until hot and crisp.

*Sun Tak
Chun Geun*

Sun Tak Spring Rolls

Sun Tak, a suburban town just outside of Canton, is the place where I was born. When I was young, this was the spring roll as far as I was concerned. Our spring rolls are simpler in content than the Cantonese spring rolls, but surely as delicious. Notice that the cooking technique is quite different too. These spring rolls stay in my memory for other reasons as well; it seems I was always the person to prepare the bean sprouts, a tedious chore that meant I had to snap off both ends, then stack them so they could be cooked, not a pleasant job for these wonderful ngan jum, *"silver needles." Maybe it was worth the effort.*

	3 ounces shrimp, washed, shelled, deveined, shredded
Marinade for Shrimp	¹/₈ teaspoon salt
	¹/₈ teaspoon light soy sauce
	¹/₈ teaspoon sugar
To Continue Recipe	2 ounces fresh pork, shredded
Marinade for Pork	¹/₂ teaspoon salt
	¹/₄ teaspoon light soy sauce
To Finish the Dish	1 tablespoon peanut oil
	3 scallions, ends discarded, cut into 1¹/₂-inch pieces, white portions shredded
	1 pound bean sprouts, washed, drained, patted dry
	12 spring roll skins
	1 egg, beaten
	5 cups peanut oil (for deep-frying)

Makes 12 spring rolls

1. Combine the shrimp marinade ingredients and add shrimp. Mix well and allow to stand for 30 minutes in reserve. Combine the

pork marinade ingredients and add the pork. Mix well and allow to stand for 30 minutes in reserve.

2. Heat wok over high heat for 30 seconds. Add 1 tablespoon of peanut oil and coat wok with spatula. When a wisp of white smoke appears, add pork and its marinade. Stir and cook for 20 seconds. Add shrimp and its marinade, stir, and cook for 10 seconds. Add scallions and stir in, cooking for 30 seconds. Add bean sprouts. Mix and cook for about 1 minute, until sprouts wilt. Turn off heat. Place in a strainer and allow to drain over a bowl. Stir occasionally with chopsticks to help drainage.

3. Make the spring rolls: Place 2 tablespoons of filling in a line across one end of the skin. Dip your fingers in the beaten egg and wet edges of skin. Fold over tip, and continue to roll, folding in sides as you do. Keep rubbing beaten egg at edges to ensure spring roll will be sealed. Repeat until all spring rolls are made.

4. Deep-fry in 5 cups of peanut oil at 325°F (in three batches) until golden brown, 3 to 4 minutes. Keep turning spring rolls to ensure even color. Remove from oil, drain, and serve immediately.

Serving Suggestion: As with Cantonese Spring Rolls, I like Vinegar Ginger Dip (page 45) or chili sauce with these.

Note: Sun Tak Spring Rolls cannot be frozen.

Shanghai
Chun Geun

Shanghai Spring Rolls

This Shanghai version of the classic spring roll of Canton is very special. People in Shanghai make these spring rolls to celebrate the New Year and welcome the spring, as do the Cantonese. But they regard the shape and color of the roll as significant, for to them it is like a gum tiu, *or "gold bar," a symbol of prosperity.*

	3 ounces fresh pork, shredded
	6 shrimp, shelled, deveined, washed, dried, shredded (2 ounces)
Marinade Ingredients	1/2 teaspoon light soy sauce
	1/4 teaspoon salt
	3/4 teaspoon sugar
	1/2 teaspoon sesame oil
	Pinch of white pepper
	1/2 teaspoon cornstarch
	1/2 teaspoon Shao-Hsing wine or sherry
Sauce Ingredients	1 1/2 teaspoons light soy sauce
	3/4 teaspoon sugar
	1/2 teaspoon sesame oil
	1 1/2 teaspoons Shao-Hsing wine or sherry
	2 tablespoons cornstarch
	1/3 cup Chicken Broth (page 33)
	Pinch of white pepper
To Continue the Recipe	5 cups cold water
	1 teaspoon salt
	3/4 pound Tientsin bok choy, cut lengthwise, then in 1/4-inch slices (4 cups, tightly packed)
To Finish the Dish	1 1/2 tablespoons peanut oil
	15 spring roll skins
	1 egg, beaten
	5 cups peanut oil (for deep-frying)

Makes 15 spring rolls

1. Combine the marinade ingredients and add the pork and shrimp. Allow to stand for 30 minutes in reserve. Combine the sauce ingredients. Reserve.

2. In a pot place the cold water and 1 teaspoon of salt. Bring to a boil over high heat. Add Tientsin bok choy. Submerge, stir, and cook for 40 seconds. Turn off heat, run cold water into pot, and drain. Repeat. Allow the bok choy to strain for 20 minutes, loosening occasionally with chopsticks to aid drainage. Reserve.

3. Heat wok over high heat for 30 seconds. Add 1½ tablespoons of peanut oil and coat wok with spatula. When a wisp of white smoke appears, add shrimp and pork mixture, with marinade. Spread in a thin layer. Cook for 30 seconds then turn over and mix. When pork and shrimp change color, add bok choy. Mix well and cook for 1 minute. Make a well in the center, stir sauce, and pour in. Mix thoroughly until sauce bubbles and thickens. Turn off heat and transfer to a shallow dish. Allow to come to room temperature. Refrigerate for 4 hours or overnight, covered.

4. Make the spring rolls: Place 2 tablespoons of filling in a line across one corner of the skin. Dip your fingers in the beaten egg and wet edges of skin. Fold over tip, and continue to roll, folding in sides as you do. Keep rubbing beaten egg at edges to ensure spring roll will be sealed. Repeat until all spring rolls are made.

5. Deep-fry in 5 cups of peanut oil at 325°F (in four batches) until golden brown, 3 to 4 minutes. Keep turning spring rolls to ensure even color. Remove from oil, drain, and serve immediately.

Serving Suggestion: I suggest no accompaniment to these spring rolls.

Note: Shanghai Spring Rolls can be frozen after cooking. To reheat, either deep-fry lightly (at 325°F) for 1 minute, or heat in a 375°F oven for 3 minutes on a side, until hot and crisp.

Saw Choi Chun Geun

Vegetable Spring Rolls

This spring roll filled only with vegetables is an example of temple food. Buddhists will eat spring rolls, but not traditional ones filled with pork or shrimp. So these are made. Usually such spring rolls contain scallions, mushrooms, and any vegetables that are fresh and crisp. This is a modern version; I add my steamed mushrooms and sun-dried tomatoes to them, for their distinct tastes. This is a most unusual spring roll.

$3/4$ pound cabbage, washed, dried, cut into $1/4$-inch pieces across ($4^1/2$ cups tightly packed)

5 cups cold water

1 teaspoon salt

$1/2$ teaspoon baking soda

4 Chinese black mushrooms, steamed (page 166), thinly sliced ($1/2$ cup)

6 sun-dried tomatoes, washed in warm water, thinly sliced ($1/3$ cup)

Paste Ingredients

$1^1/2$ tablespoons cornstarch mixed with $1^1/2$ tablespoons cold water

$1/2$ cup boiling water

Sauce Ingredients

$1^1/2$ tablespoons oyster sauce

1 teaspoon light soy sauce

1 teaspoon sugar

1 teaspoon sesame oil

$1^1/2$ teaspoons Shao-Hsing wine or sherry

2 tablespoons cornstarch

Pinch of white pepper

$1/2$ cup cold water

To Finish the Dish

$1^1/2$ tablespoons peanut oil

1 tablespoon minced young ginger, or $1^1/2$ teaspoons regular ginger

16 spring roll skins

5 cups peanut oil (for deep-frying)

Makes 16 spring rolls

1. Water blanch the cabbage: In a large pot place the 5 cups of cold water, 1 teaspoon salt, and baking soda and over high heat bring to a boil. Add the cabbage, submerge, and stir, allow to cook for 40 seconds. Turn off heat. Run cold water into pot, drain. Repeat, allow to drain for 20 minutes. Loosen cabbage occasionally with chopsticks to aid drainage. Reserve.

2. Make the paste: Place the cornstarch-water mixture and the boiling water in a small bowl and mix with a pair of chopsticks to make a smooth paste. Reserve. Mix sauce ingredients. Reserve.

3. Heat wok over high heat for 40 seconds. Add the 1½ tablespoons of peanut oil and coat wok with spatula. When a wisp of white smoke appears add the minced ginger. Stir, then add mushrooms. Stir, then add cabbage. Mix well and cook for 2 minutes. Add the sun-dried tomatoes and stir into mix. Make a well in the center, stir the sauce, and pour in. Stir well; when sauce thickens and bubbles, turn off heat. Transfer to a shallow dish and allow to come to room temperature. Refrigerate overnight, covered.

4. Make the spring rolls: Place 2 tablespoons of filling in a line across one corner of the skin. Brush the edges of the skin with the paste mixture. Fold over tip and continue to roll, folding in sides as you do. Keep brushing edges of skin with paste to ensure that spring roll will be sealed. Repeat until all spring rolls are made.

5. Deep-fry in 5 cups of peanut oil at 325°F (in four batches) until golden brown, 3 to 4 minutes. Keep turning spring rolls to ensure even color. Remove from oil, drain, and serve immediately.

Serving Suggestion: I suggest no accompaniment with these Vegetable Spring Rolls. The sun-dried tomatoes and the steamed mushrooms provide sufficient flavor.

Note: Vegetable Spring Rolls can be frozen after cooking. To reheat, either deep-fry lightly (at 325°F) for 1 minute, or heat in a preheated 375°F oven for 3 minutes on a side, until hot and crisp.

Note: The reason for the use of a paste instead of beaten egg is because these rolls must be totally vegetarian. Often, however, people have adverse reactions to eggs. If this is so, then use the paste as a substitute in any of the recipes.

Ging Hei
Lai Mut

Surprise Packages

Here is my variation on the theme of the spring roll—thoroughly new "Surprise Packages" shaped quite like those party noisemakers that pop when they are pulled. The Chinese words for these rolls, ging hei lai mut, translate as "happy surprise gift," and so they are. These can be marvelous hors d'oeuvres, if you wish, or can be eaten as you would any other spring roll. As I have noted earlier, this recipe uses the thicker, yellowish egg roll skins.

　4　cups Chicken Broth (page 33)
　1　pound of well-trimmed filet mignon, cut
　　　　along the grain into strips 2 inches long
　　　　and $\frac{1}{2}$ inch wide
　3　scallions, cut into $1\frac{1}{2}$-inch pieces, white
　　　　portions quartered lengthwise
$1\frac{1}{2}$　tablespoons finely shredded ginger
　12　sun-dried tomatoes, packed in oil, cut into
　　　　thin strips
　$\frac{1}{2}$　teaspoon salt
　6　egg roll skins, square
　4　cups peanut oil (for deep-frying)

Makes 24 surprise packages

1. In a medium pot bring chicken broth to a boil over high heat. Add the beef strips, cook for 3 seconds, and remove from heat. Cover the pan and let stand for 1 minute. Strain immediately. (Reserve the stock for another use if you wish.) Let the beef cool to room temperature.

2. In a bowl combine the beef, scallions, ginger, sun-dried tomatoes, and salt. Toss to mix well.

3. For the surprise packages: Cut each egg roll skin into 4 equal squares. Place a piece of beef, about 4 pieces of scallion, several shreds of ginger, and strips of sun-dried tomato in the center of each wrapper. Moisten the two edges of the wrapper that parallel the direction in which the beef lies. Pick up these edges and squeeze between your thumb and index finger to seal. Fold

seam down to tighten into a cylinder. The package will resemble
a log with both ends open. Twist each end gently, but firmly, to
seal completely in the shape of a firecracker.

4. Heat a wok over high heat for 40 seconds. Add the peanut oil
   and heat to 350°F. In small batches, without crowding, slide
   the packages into the hot oil and deep-fry, turning frequently,
   until crisp and golden brown all over, 4 to 5 minutes. Remove
   with a slotted spoon, drain on paper towels, and serve hot,
   immediately.

Serving Suggestion: A few drops of Red Oil (page 44)
enhances these Surprise Packages nicely.

Note: These may be frozen after frying. If you plan to do so,
cook them only for half the specified time, or until they are
light brown. To serve, defrost all and return to room temperature, then refry in oil at 340°F until golden brown, 2 to 2½
minutes.

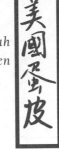

Mei Guah
Dan Guen

American Egg Rolls

This is truly a creation of that hybrid, the Chinese-American restaurant. There is nothing like the American Egg Roll in China, that loglike cylinder filled mostly with shredded cabbage. What the Chinese would call an egg roll would be like a spring roll, small and delicate. Of the various fillings, one of them would always be well-fried scrambled eggs, cut up into strips. It is, however, possible to create a fine egg roll that will look like the American sort, but will have a Chinese heritage, and here it is.

> 5 cups cold water
> 1 slice of ginger, 1 inch thick, lightly smashed
> 1 large garlic clove, peeled
> 1 medium onion, cut into ¼-inch dice
> 1 tablespoon plus 1½ teaspoons sugar
> 2½ teaspoons salt
> 6 medium shrimp (¼ pound) shelled, deveined, washed
>   2-pound head of green cabbage, tough outer leaves removed, halved, cored, finely chopped (6 cups)
> ¼ pound Roast Pork (page 121) cut into ¼-inch dice
> 12 egg roll skins, as specified
> 1 egg, beaten
> 4 cups peanut oil (for deep-frying)

Makes 12 egg rolls

1. Place cold water in a large pot. Add ginger, garlic, sugar, onion, and salt and bring to a boil over high heat. Add the shrimp and cook until they curl and turn pink, about 1 minute. Discard the garlic and ginger and, using a slotted spoon or Chinese strainer, transfer the shrimp to a sieve to drain. Allow to cool slightly, then cut into ¼-inch dice. Reserve.

2. Bring the water in the pot back to a boil over high heat. Put in the cabbage and cook until the cabbage turns bright green, about

1½ minutes. Drain thoroughly through a strainer and set aside to cool slightly. Press down to remove any excess water from cabbage.

3. In a large bowl, combine the shrimp and the Roast Pork and season with salt to taste. Add the vegetables and mix together well. Divide filling into 12 equal portions.

4. Place an egg roll skin on a work surface like a diamond, with a tip facing you. Place one portion of the filling in a horizontal line across the bottom third of the skin, then fold the tip closest to you over the filling toward the center. Lightly brush the edges of the skin with beaten egg, then fold them into the center. Brush the surface with egg. Fold toward you to seal the cylinder. Repeat with remaining wrappers and filling until all egg rolls are made.

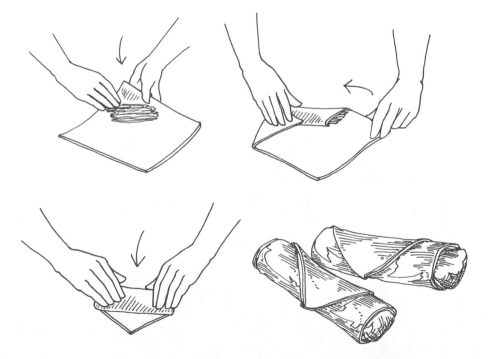

5. Heat wok over high heat for 40 seconds. Add the 4 cups of peanut oil and heat to 350°F. Cook in three batches of 4. Add

the egg rolls to the wok and fry, turning frequently to ensure even color, 4 to 5 minutes. Remove to a strainer and allow to drain. Repeat with all egg rolls until done. Serve immediately.

Serving Suggestion: These are complemented well with some Hot Mustard (page 41).

Note: These egg rolls should not be frozen. They will keep, refrigerated, for 3 days. To reheat, deep-fry in 350°F oil for slightly more than 1 minute, until hot and crisp.

Ho Ho Sik

A Few Last Words

It is my hope that not only have you enjoyed my book, but you have used it, and that you will *continue* to use and enjoy it. Although it is a cookbook, it represents an aspect of the Chinese kitchen imbued with custom, tradition, and history. It tells you a bit of how the Chinese live, and have lived, what they believe, and something about their teahouses and teas. Most importantly, however, I hope I have provided you some sense of the ever-changing nature, the vigor, and the adaptability of Chinese cooking in general and of the teahouse in particular, as well as the deep respect for good food that is so much a part of Chinese life.

Ho ho sik. Good Eating.

Index

American Egg Rolls, 190–92

Baked Bun Dough, 132
    recipes with, 133–39
Baked Chicken Buns, 138–39
Baked Curry Pork Buns, 136–37
Baked Pork Buns, 133–35
Bamboo shoots, 22
    recipes with, 52–53, 56–59,
        70–71, 74–75, 126–27,
        138–39, 153–55, 158, 178–80
Basic Shrimp Filling, 158
    recipes with, 159–65
Bean curd, 22–23
    recipe with, 162–63
    See also Soybean cake
Bean sprouts, 23
    recipe with, 181–82
Beef, recipes with, 78–79, 144–45,
    188–89
Beijing
    breads of, 115
    Pearl Balls in, 142
Black beans, fermented, 23
    recipe with, 146–47
Blanching, 18

Bok choy, 23
    recipes with, 78–79, 86–91
    See also Tientsin bok choy
Buns
    dough for, 117, 132
    recipes for, 92–94, 118–31,
      133–39

Cantonese cuisine, 1, 4, 8–11, 141,
    157, 173
    recipes of, 60–63, 82–83, 95–97,
      113–14, 118–20, 122–23,
      146–47, 151–55, 170–71,
      178–83
    steamed and baked buns in,
      115–16
Cantonese Spring Rolls, 178–80
Chicken, recipes with, 71–72, 80–83,
    106–8, 126–27, 138–39
Chicken Broth, 33
Chicken *Soi Gau*, 80–81
Chinese black mushrooms, 24
    recipes with, 56–59, 66–67,
      111–12, 126–29, 138–39,
      148–55, 164–67, 185–87
"Chinese cabbage." *See* Bok choy